HOW TO MAKE MONEY IN REAL ESTATE IN THE NEW ECONOMY

Matthew Martinez

New York   Chicago   San Francisco   Lisbon   London
Madrid   Mexico City   Milan   New Delhi   San Juan
Seoul   Singapore   Sydney   Toronto

The **McGraw·Hill** Companies

1 2 3 4 5 6 7 8 9 0   DOC/DOC   1 9 8 7 6 5 4 3 2 1 0

ISBN: 978-0-07-174262-7
MHID: 0-07-174262-X

This publication is designed to provide accurate and authoritative information in regard to the subject matter covered. It is sold with the understanding that neither the author nor the publisher is engaged in rendering legal, accounting, or other professional service. If legal advice or other expert assistance is required, the services of a competent professional person should be sought.

> —From a Declaration of Principles Jointly Adopted by a Committee of the American Bar Association and a Committee of Publishers and Associations

Library of Congress Cataloging-in-Publication Data

Martinez, Matthew A.
   How to make money in real estate in the new economy / by Matthew Martinez.
      p.   cm.
   Includes index.
   ISBN 978-0-07-174262-7 (alk. paper)
   1. Real estate investment—United States.
   2. United States—Economic conditions—2009 I. Title.

   HD255.M37153 2011
   332.63'240973—dc22   2010025373

McGraw-Hill books are available at special quantity discounts to use as premiums and sales promotions, or for use in corporate training programs. To contact a representative, please visit the Contact Us pages at www.mhprofessional.com.

This book is printed on acid-free paper.

This book is dedicated to my son, Alec.

Perhaps Victor Frankl described it best in his marvelous book, *Man's Search for Meaning*:

> Love is the ultimate and the highest goal to which man can aspire. The salvation of man is through love . . . man who has nothing left in this world still may know bliss, be it only for a brief moment, in the contemplation of his beloved.

How wonderful my life has become since you've entered this world . . . I love you with all of my heart.

Papa

xoxo TQM

Contents

Contents

Preface

When the economy slows, most people stop investing in real estate and wait until economic conditions improve before getting back into the market. These individuals perceive a downturn in the economy as a clear indication to stop buying. Contrary to popular belief, periods of extreme crisis in the real estate sector actually provide investors with a greater opportunity to generate significant wealth. If you have an entrepreneurial spirit and the conviction to persevere during uncertain times, now could be the very best moment in your life to act. In fact, most of the experienced real estate investors I know are salivating at the prospect of making more money in these "tough" times—more money than they've ever made in the past. The current market conditions are quite favorable for acquiring great properties at prices we haven't seen in more then 20 years.

In turbulent times, however, innovation is the key to success and the means for greater prosperity. Indeed, the current global financial crisis mandates change. Real estate entrepreneurs must learn how to thrive—not just survive—in this new economy. Just getting by and weathering the storm should not be the end goal. Battered by declining values, higher vacancies, and frozen credit markets, many real estate entrepreneurs these days are, indeed, fighting for their very survival. But opportunities abound for the savvy investor. Cap rates on stable investment properties have increased dramatically. Bank-owned properties in good locations are being liquidated at rock-bottom prices. The inability to refinance debt presents even more opportunities for acquiring good real estate assets at very attractive prices. It's the perfect storm for investors who want to get started building their portfolio or for those who already own real estate but want to expand their holdings and cash flow.

Preface

How to Make Money in Real Estate in the New Economy is not just another book about making a fortune in real estate by scooping up distressed assets during a period of economic crisis. Rather, this book's principal theme emphasizes the necessity of reinventing one's business and self during any challenging economic period. It's about thinking and acting in a way that will cultivate success, even when everyone else is running scared. This book is about having your most profitable year when most others are planning for bankruptcy. It's about taking advantage of today's poor economic climate and finding a way to profit from it.

Numerous books today painstakingly describe how to acquire real estate through short sales, auctions, Real Estate Owned assets, note sales, and so on. This book, however, is not a duplication of what currently exists on the shelves of your local bookstores. Instead, I consciously avoided what had already been written ad nauseam about distressed real estate and wrote a new kind of book that shows how successful real estate entrepreneurs (who embraced change and modified their behavior) could make money during "challenging" times. Throughout this book, you'll read about real life examples of fortunes made and lost during this epic time—a new time (in fact, a new economy) that is still in its infancy, but that still offers tremendous opportunity to those with initiative, perseverance, and optimism.

Having spent the past few years in the trenches of the distressed markets of southern Florida (aka: ground zero), the Midwest, and New England, I share throughout this book what I have seen, learned, and personally experienced.

Moreover, readers of my other books expressed their appreciation for sharing my experiences with them in first-person prose. They enjoyed reading about my real-life stories because they could personally relate to them and understand them through my unique perspective. I didn't want to stray too far from the formula that made my first two books such a tremendous success, so you'll notice a similar writing style here.

Preface

That being said, this book addresses several problems that I feel are endemic in many real estate titles being offered today:

- *Problem:* People these days don't have the time or inclination to read a 500-page novel. Most real estate books are far too long and provide too much detailed information.
- *Solution:* This isn't cold fusion, so simplification and brevity were chosen over complexity and exacting detail. Each chapter is relatively short (typically fewer than 2,000 words) and specific to a particular idea or concept. This book provides an overview of a series of diverse topics that should interest almost every investor. Hopefully, the result is a readable book for individuals who prefer less granular detail but still want an ample review.

- *Problem:* Many real estate books are written by journalists or ghostwriters who have no practical experience in the field.
- *Solution:* I have been actively involved in real estate since the 1990s. Moreover, my vocational endeavors include apartment buildings (multifamily), shopping centers (retail), office buildings, property development and management, leasing, and brokerage. I am an active professional in the field, dedicating 100 percent of my professional time to the real estate industry. This is also my third book on real estate investing since 2005.

- *Problem:* Real estate books are seldom written in the first person and don't provide real-life examples of successes and failures.
- *Solution:* This book is filled with real stories from the trenches. The good, bad, and ugly of real estate investing are highlighted throughout this book. Moreover, I've included compelling stories from other investors who were willing to share their unique, personal stories with you.

Preface

It's a proven fact that money can be made during good times or bad. During times like today, however, it will take more creativity than the average Joe has to succeed. Then again, there's a lot less competition with fewer amateurs mucking up the field and artificially driving up prices.

The following is an e-mail sent to me from a highly respected and astute real estate investor who has written more than 10 books on the subject. I'm sharing this correspondence with you because it succinctly summarizes the current state of the market.

> Matt: Personally, last year was the best year I've ever had, and this year is going to top last. We are currently in the greatest time I've seen in my lifetime for true investors. I've bought 15 new properties since February and have offers outstanding on six more at this time. Some of the deals I'm getting are unbelievable. I realize the economy is terrible for speculators, but for true investors I don't see how things could get much better. FINALLY, we are able to find numerous properties at prices where the numbers make sense.

Naturally, when the real estate market collapsed, most investors were reluctant to make new acquisitions—even when the fundamentals of investing were finally turning in their favor. After enduring a decade in which an overheated market made it impossible to find profitable deals, there is now an abundance of real estate opportunities available. Value can be extracted from the downturn via opportunistic acquisitions and patient, methodical investing—assuming, of course, that you know what to look for and how to find it.

Opportunities will abound in the new economy. Though the economic conditions remain unfavorable for those who commonly see the glass as being half empty rather than half full, there is a limitless treasure

Preface

trove of deals to pursue for those who are more sanguine about the prospect of succeeding during the absence of rapid economic growth. Now is your time to act!

Acknowledgments

There are several individuals I'd like to thank for making this book a reality. After all, one doesn't work in a vacuum; it takes a team effort to write, edit, edit again, publish, and market a 35,000-word document!

First and foremost, I'd like to thank my editor, Mary Glenn, for considering me (one year ago) for this opportunity. I truly appreciate your support, guidance, and partnership during the past seven years. I'd also like to extend a debt of gratitude to Tania Loghmani, Scott Kurtz, and Cheryl Hudson, who work tirelessly behind the scenes at McGraw-Hill.

My family has always been a tremendous source of inspiration and pride to me. I'd like to thank each of them for their support through the years: Alec, Nico, Lisa, Nubia, Mom, Dad, Becky, Joey, Jonathan, Wendy, Ethan, Ben, Noah, and Fr. Jack.

Special thanks to my wife, Lisa, for picking up the "loose ends" during the 10 months it took to write this book. TQM

Part 1

The Past

1

Understanding the Housing Crisis

It was a hot, humid day in Miami, Florida. I was running a few minutes late, so I quickly knocked on the door of unit 205. A gentleman in his early seventies greeted me and politely asked, "Sr. Martinez, como estás?" His facial features, mannerisms, and tone exuded experience—a man who had spent decades in the real estate trenches, a veteran who had survived numerous downturns and volatile market cycles over the past 50-plus years. I remember telling myself, "This guy has probably seen it all!" But I knew those profoundly deep wrinkles around his eyes weren't caused solely by vocational stress; rather, they were indicative of a man who enjoyed spending much of his free time navigating the waterways from Biscayne Bay to the Florida Keys aboard multimillion-dollar yachts. In other words, this guy had worked hard for many decades but had also managed to survive and financially prosper in this cutthroat business.

The Past

Unfortunately, this particular day was different. Even a man with five decades of real estate experience had never experienced anything like the current market conditions. And that's where this story begins.

With a handshake still quite powerful for a man of his age, he greeted me and asked that I take a seat in his makeshift office—known as unit 205.

"Matt, I'm telling you this is just bad luck. Seven months after we acquired this apartment complex and converted it to condos, we had 132 units (out of slightly more than 200 total units) under agreement. We would have been able to pay off all the outstanding loans after selling those condos. The remaining 80 units (assuming they were sold after the first phase of sales) represented pure profit. In all my years in this business, I've never seen a market change so quickly. It simply fell off a cliff. Even if we were able to find willing and able buyers, they simply can't get the required financing nowadays. The credit markets have all dried up. It's a disaster, and we're bleeding more than \$12,000 a day! We haven't paid the mortgage on the property in four months; the complex is only 50 percent occupied, and our loan officer has flagged our file and transferred it to the special assets department at the bank. Believe it or not, this was our very last project. My business partner and I were going to retire after this one. Matt, can you help us?"

This is just one example from dozens of similar conversations I've had with developers since 2007. The range of financial and psychological "pain" spanned the full spectrum, but the ominous undertones always remained the same. With the housing market in a free fall, property owners, investors, speculators, and developers were left struggling under highly leveraged mortgages they couldn't afford, given that their properties were no longer worth what they had originally paid for them. As the amount of nonperforming loans escalated, lenders began to falter under the weight of too much bad debt. This chain of events served as a catalyst for the global financial crisis that began in 2008.

The subprime mortgage debacle, subsequent credit crunch, financial meltdown, and global recession have not only decimated investors' wealth but have forever altered the landscape of real estate investing as we know it. Heavy mortgage losses forced banks to immediately restrict lending, which caused real estate sales volumes to precipitously drop as prospective buyers, investors, and even speculators awaited the bottom of the market before they would consider reentry.

The credit crisis, ensuing recession, and double-digit unemployment dragged real estate markets into the worst recession we've seen in decades. Property value losses, rising foreclosures, higher vacancies, and restricted capital markets are the norm and not the exception these days. Without a doubt, we are experiencing troubled economic times for all real estate investors who overpaid, overleveraged, and didn't anticipate the fall.

Government's Role

The housing crisis was exacerbated by the government's role in encouraging home buying. In fact, the American dream demanded home ownership, and the federal government was in the business of making those dreams possible. American citizens were led to believe that they would not achieve that dream without home ownership. One of the primary goals of both the Clinton and Bush II administrations was to dramatically increase the rate of homeownership in our country. The government-sponsored entities (GSEs), including Fannie Mae and Freddie Mac, were told to expand the number of home loans to low-income individuals—otherwise known as subprime borrowers. Individuals who really could not afford the costs of a house were suddenly able to buy much more than they could handle. Access to cheap, easy money made it possible for millions of renters to become property owners. This experiment led to the subprime mortgage crisis.

During the winter of 2008, I met with Congressman Barney Frank, chairman of the House Financial Services Committee, in his local office in Massachusetts. We discussed the economic and housing crisis, and what needed to be done. He declared his strong support for affordable housing (he always had been a staunch advocate for providing more affordable housing), but also expressed his opinion that millions of families should have continued renting and that it should not be the government's goal to encourage homeownership to those who cannot afford it. Rep. Frank said, "Not everyone should be a homeowner. In fact, there are a lot of people who should have remained renters."

Collateralized Mortgage Obligations (CMOs)

By 2001, the dot-com bubble imploded, and investors fled the tech market in droves. They considered real estate a safer place to invest, so billions of dollars were diverted to real estate investment vehicles. Investment banks created collateralized mortgage obligations (CMOs) to capture these investment dollars. CMOs are a type of mortgage-backed security (MBS) whereby bonds (sold to investors) represent claims to the cash flows from pools of mortgages. They essentially served as a means to securitize large amounts of mortgages so investors could purchase them and fund the boom.

With increased demand for CMOs, lenders reduced their lending standards, and the subprime market flourished. Investment banks were enamored of CMOs, and they invested billions. However, when property owners—under the heavy weight of their loans—began to default, investment banks, local and regional banks, and other financial institutions quickly shuttered. These events led to a national financial crisis not experienced in the modern era.

Appreciating Values

Before the crash, most property owners expected the appreciation of their properties to continue unabated and that double-digit annual increases would last forever. Interest rates remained extremely low after the tech implosion, so debt was affordable. Lenders began to market exotic mortgages such as negative amortization loans (pay the minimum required, and the principal could increase). Credit was plentiful, and NINJA (no income, no job, no assets) loans were common. Exotic loans to subprime borrowers (people who had poor credit) were regularly approved, but everyone knew they couldn't sustain the heavy debt burden indefinitely. In other words, almost anyone could and did get a mortgage to buy real estate that he or she could not afford. Waiters, for example, who were making $30,000 a year were buying $1.5 million condos!

Appraisers worked closely with mortgage brokers and lenders to ensure that property values were in line with the sales price. Values were rising so quickly that no one could really estimate true market value. Most lenders just sold their portfolios of loans to the secondary market, so there was little risk. If they made the loan, they'd collect their fee from the borrower, earn additional fees from selling the loan to the secondary market, and have zero risk on their balance sheet. It was the perfect scenario for housing arbitrage, and our country's finest minds working at our most prestigious financial institutions made a fortune.

Homeowners leveraged their property's equity by extracting every penny out of it through home equity loans. They used the additional capital on spending sprees that included expensive cars, vacation homes, exotic travel, sophisticated electronics, and so on. Eventually, real estate values stopped going up, and homeowners found themselves left with multiple loans on properties that were not worth what they owed on them. They were left with negative equity and little incentive to continue paying the mortgage.

Today's Environment

Property values have declined significantly since the bubble burst. Many property owners owe more on their homes than they are currently worth. With stricter lending practices adopted by banks, homeowners are unable to refinance their properties to 30-year fixed rates because they are under water with no residual equity remaining. Banks won't lend more than the real estate is worth, so a lot of property owners find themselves between the proverbial rock and a hard place.

The investing strategies practiced just a few years ago (during the boom years) are now terribly inadequate for succeeding in today's distressed real estate market. Investors need to think and act differently if they want to survive this down cycle and profit when the economy eventually rebounds.

While fully recognizing the mistakes of the past and providing sound advice for taking advantage of future opportunities, this book explains how to successfully invest in today's distressed market. Recent developments have crushed many real estate speculators, but they have also created profitable new opportunities for individuals willing to serve as the next generation of contrarian investors—a generation that will undoubtedly make their fortunes by buying when everyone else is desperately selling. This book offers effective strategies for taking advantage of this new era of investing. Though most of yesterday's most favored strategies no longer work, today's savvy real estate investors can still find great opportunities for growth and profit—if, of course, they acknowledge how recent events are altering the real estate landscape and if they determine how to take full advantage of the situation.

Investors must return to the sound fundamentals that have worked for centuries. It's back to "blocking and tackling" and doing what has consistently worked in the past—buying on cash flow and disregarding the notion of automatic price appreciation. Increases in value during this tough cycle will be dependent on your property's Net Operating Income. You can't do much about the economy, so you must add value. Buying at distressed and greatly depreciated prices is a good start. If you're going to make money in real estate during these challenging times—you'll have to earn it the hard way!

What's to Come Next?

A reset has occurred in our new economy. Real estate values will reset lower. Deleveraging is taking place. Debt-to-equity ratios will become more manageable. Only people with very good credit will have access to new loans, but they'll need to put significantly more money down to buy.

Real estate investors should expect a wave of foreclosures on over-leveraged properties to continue during this year. That being said, I anticipate single-family homes and rental apartments to be on the forefront of a recovery. A reduction in construction will limit supply while demand rises because of immigration, retiring baby boomers, and 80 million echo boomers leaving college to enter the workforce (more on that later in the book). Office and retail will falter from 2011 to 2012. But, once again, tremendous financial opportunity can always be found during distressed cycles.

In the postcrisis landscape, success in real estate will be defined by an unwavering concentration on the fundamentals—valuing properties based on their existing merits coupled with a realistic approach to determining both the current and future financial potential of a given asset.

2

Overleveraged

Leverage

---

lev-er-age: the use of a small initial investment, credit, or borrowed funds to gain a very high return in relation to one's investment, to control a much larger investment, or to reduce one's own liability for any loss.

Source: Dictionary.com

Before the Great Depression, banks required a 50 percent down payment from creditworthy borrowers before approving an application for a real estate loan. Mortgages were then typically paid back within the next 10 years.

The Past

In vast contrast to the lending standards widely accepted at the turn of the twentieth century, we spent the next 80 years growing accustomed to less-restrictive lending practices. In particular, during the boom years, easy credit and minimal lending restrictions were the norm: 100 percent financing with zero down, 30-year amortization schedules, and mortgage processing that did not require applicants to have a source of income or a history of good credit. Banks used seductively low introductory interest rates to hypnotize the nation into borrowing more than it needed.

The temptation to use less of your own money and more of the bank's to buy real estate was insatiable during the past eight years. Most speculators couldn't resist the allure of cheap and abundant sources of debt to fuel their acquisition binges. One overleveraged investor once told me, "It was as if I were playing a game of Monopoly, and I was using money that wasn't quite real. They were obliged to give it to me, and I was obliged to take it." Ultimately, investors who were more conservative and able to demonstrate financial constraint (i.e., investors who refrained from being overleveraged) will thrive during this downturn and likely become even stronger when the economy fully rebounds.

The object of the speculative real estate game was to quickly buy buy buy during the boom. Inasmuch as the banks were fighting for your business, "extreme leverage" became an acceptable way of making acquisitons and admittedly the only way to really close deals at overly inflated prices if you didn't have the cash reserves on hand to self-finance a larger portion of the purchase price.

How could investors continue to pay these exorbitant prices and finance the vast majority of their purchases when they had so much debt? How could banks lend money on income-producing properties that had absolutely no chance of generating a positive cash flow? How could this possibly have been permitted?

Not only was it allowed, but it was encouraged because everyone seemed to believe that property values would continue to rise. Logically, then, rents would also continue to rise. If revenue rose and values kept pace, then the existing debt would not pose a problem because equity would rise along with property values. No problem, right? Well, when the bubble finally burst, equity quickly dissipated, rents declined, and values dropped like a rock. With properties worth less than the debt owed on them, owners began to lose confidence in the future value of their investments. Suddenly, homeowners, speculators, and investors of income-producing properties stopped making mortgage payments.

Deleveraging

> de lev er age: The reduction of financial instruments or borrowed capital previously used to increase the potential return of an investment. It is the opposite of *leverage*.
>
> *Source:* Dictionary.com

As deleveraging (also know as a "resetting") occurs, a more balanced market for the entire real estate sector will result. If property owners pay down debt by making additional equity payments, loan-to-value (LTV) ratios (based on current appraisals) will decrease to acceptable figures.

Property owners who want to refinance and have ample cash reserves for additional equity payments will need to pay down their mortgage balances to achieve an acceptable LTV ratio before their lenders agree to refinance.

If property owners lack sufficient cash reserves to pay down their debt, their note is maturing, and they can't keep up with the monthly payments or refinance, then the only other option may be foreclosure, unless the lender can be convinced to extend the loan or consider alternative exit strategies.

If your properties are not overleveraged but they lost significant equity in the downturn and the LTV is tight but the property generates a positive income stream, then you will likely survive the downturn if you can be patient.

If your property is in the red (negative cash flow), then you'll have to come "out of pocket" each month to pay the expenses not covered by the property's income stream. Otherwise, you can dispose of the property—assuming you can sell it for at least the amount owed and pay off the existing note. Or you can sell it for less than the amount owed (a short sale) or simply hand the keys back to the bank through what's known as a deed in lieu of foreclosure.

Case Study 1

Gaston Safar, a friend of mine who lives in Boston, started cutting hair at a young age while he was living in France. He moved to Boston with his family when he was 20, and one year later he opened Safar Coiffure with his two brothers. Almost three decades later, Safar Coiffure is known as one of the very best salons in Beantown. The name Safar is equally legendary for the private investment group he established to buy and sell real estate along trendy Newbury Street in the Back Bay.

Gaston was reared in relative poverty, so after arriving in the United States, he worked 7 days a week, 15 hours a day. He worked three different jobs (the salon, Baskin-Robbins, and carpentry) so he wouldn't have to return to a life of poverty. "I had no safety net, and knew that I couldn't afford to make any mistakes because no one was there to help me."

Although Gaston came from humble beginnings, he was a real visionary investor. After saving for several years, he bought the entire building where his salon was located. "I didn't want to pay rent and make my landlord any richer than he already was," he quipped. He saved his money, lived a meager lifestyle, and never bought a building with more than 50 percent leverage. Once he saved enough capital, he would buy another building along Newbury Street—the central shopping district in Boston. Today, he owns more than a dozen buildings in Boston with absolutely no

Overleveraged

debt. He managed to pay off the mortgages on each of his properties. The real estate empire he built on his own during the past 40 years is now one of the most revered portfolios in town.

When I learned that the retail space on the ground floor of one of his commercial properties had been vacant for two years, I asked Gaston if he was motivated to lease it. He told me that, because he didn't have any debt on the property, he would wait patiently until he found the "right" tenant who would complement his salon. He had already rejected several prospective tenants. In other words, he wasn't in any rush.

Do you think Gaston will survive this economic meltdown? You bet your bottom dollar he will! A conservative investor who built his salon on hard work and a dedication to perfection, he did extremely well for himself. Since arriving in the United States, his primary goal was to obtain financial security and to free himself from the fear of poverty. He didn't have a specific dollar amount or a net worth in mind as his goal. Instead, he wanted to make enough money so that he wouldn't have to work by the age of 50. Fortunately for Gaston, he was able to accomplish this feat a full decade earlier—at the tender age of 40.

Gaston was never tempted to buy more than he could afford, and he never chased properties outside of Boston or Miami. After more than three decades of investing, he avoided the excesses of the past eight years and kept to his golden rule of acquiring real estate with as little debt as possible, while maximizing his portfolio's cash flow by quickly paying off his mortgages. During the "building" years, he lived in a modest apartment with his wife and kids and took few vacations. He saved his earnings and remained steadfast with his conviction of paying off mortgages. If the monthly debt service ran $3,000 a month, he would try to pay $4,000, $5,000, or $6,000.

He says that he could have owned many, many more buildings but that it wasn't worth his time to create a massive portfolio of real estate. He'd rather have a dozen well-located buildings that were debt-free than 100 buildings that were leveraged to the hilt. Today, the annual cash flow from his modest holdings provides enough passive income to allow him to do whatever he wants with the rest of his life. It couldn't have happened to a more-deserving guy!

Case Study 2

RK Associates is a privately held, family-owned real estate development company. It has a proven track record of success that spans more than 30 years. The company was founded by Raanan Katz, an industrious young man who grew up in Israel. He immigrated to the States in his early 20s with the hope of playing basketball for the Boston Celtics. Unfortunately, he was the final player let go from the Celtics that year—he was edged out by eventual Hall of Fame sixth man John Havlicek.

Raanan eventually settled in Boston and purchased small apartment buildings. During the next several years, he amassed several thousand apartment units in the greater Boston area. In 1980, he started acquiring commercial (mainly retail) buildings in Boston and South Florida. Ranaan currently owns more than 6 million square feet of commercial space in New England and Miami.

He, like Gaston, avoided excessive leverage. In fact, his conservative borrowing practices have allowed him to amass a sizable portfolio that generates a tremendous cash flow. By using minimal debt as part of his financing strategy, he guaranteed his company's growth and stability for three decades and allowed RK Associates to withstand numerous volatile market cycles.

Case Study 3

Another company based in southern Florida is the absolute antithesis of RK Associates. This one was extremely active during the past seven years—being one of the leading acquirers of real estate during the boom. Its portfolio includes more than 30 commercial properties totaling 5-plus million square feet of retail and mixed-use real estate.

Overleveraged

Unfortunately, this organization bought at the peak of the market and overpaid—using as much leverage as its lenders would allow.

It acquired properties with nearly 100 percent short-term debt (three to five years) because the organization touted its ability to increase the bottom line at its properties (even though its numbers exceeded historical performances) and quickly sell at a premium. Unfortunately, its lenders believed the organization's outlandish financial projections and provided the loans. To make matters worse, it then secured construction loans to make capital improvements to its value-add projects. It essentially used more than 100 percent financing. Its strategy was to make improvements, increase rents, maximize NOI, and sell to the highest bidder—a highly profitable model if you can get in and out while the market is still ascending. It's a terrible strategy if you can't execute before the market tanks! The organization found itself struggling under the weight of its own debt. With most of its loans set to mature, vacancies rising at its centers, and existing rents declining, this company is now on the verge of financial ruin. Unfortunately, it recently gave notice to more than half its staff and will likely file for bankruptcy before the end of the year.

All this company's properties are now in jeopardy of being seized by its lenders. I have been told it is in the midst of restructuring its existing debt, but few industry experts say that its lenders will work with the company because its situation is so dire.

During the next few years, more than $1.4 trillion worth of commercial real estate loans will mature. Experts anticipate that nearly 75 percent of these borrowers will likely default.

Bankers and Leverage

Unlike previous busts, overbuilding can't be blamed for this real estate collapse. An oversupply of money and the use of excessive leverage caused the residential and commercial real estate markets to shutter.

The Past

Bankers, in their rush to make more loans, readily accepted borrowers' growth projections and overlooked problems inherent in overleveraged assets. They were eager to make the loans, even if those loans were riddled with too much risk. Because lenders could sell the paper (in the form of securities) to investors, their risk tolerance increased. In other words, they had little financial exposure as long as they were able to sell the loans.

Primary market debt issuers made loans based on the government-sponsored enterprises' (GSEs) more lax underwriting guidelines. These banks then sold their loans to the secondary market (GSEs, intermediaries, and correspondents, including organizations such as Fannie Mae, Freddie Mac, CitiMortgage, Countrywide, Taylor Bean, GMAC, etc.) The secondary market would then package the mortgages into mortgage-backed securities and sell them to investment groups such as pension funds, insurance companies, and hedge funds. Banks were willing to make subprime loans to high-risk applicants because they would process the loans as quickly as possible and sell them off to the secondary market. The risk was virtually nonexistent from the lender's point of view because the lender was able to pass the "hot potato" to the next person in line. Unfortunately, if you were left with a bundle of bad loans when the music stopped, you found yourself with a lapful of rotten potatoes and a great deal of financial distress. As a result, I estimate that lenders will not unwind the considerable tightening on credit for many years to come.

Part 2

The Present

3

A Buyer's Market

A buyer's market is sometimes referred to as a "soft market." A buyer's market is a real estate market that tends to have more sellers than buyers, and lower prices result from the excess of supply over demand.

Prior to the economic downturn, real estate assets were overvalued and due for an enormous correction. Buyers are now successfully negotiating significant discounts on both residential and commercial real estate assets. Experts estimate that commercial real estate operating revenue is down by 30 to 40 percent; therefore, buyers are well positioned to negotiate aggressively on acquisitions. With values still falling, there has never been a better time for investors to be acquiring real estate.

After a market bubble is popped, prices don't always return to the natural equilibrium. Instead, they go past historical average levels to a point of being grossly undervalued (the bottom's bottom). During boom years, developers tend to overproduce, so there's excess inventory coming onto the market. However, consumers lose confidence in the economy after a bubble bursts. Lenders grow leery of exposing themselves to more risk, thereby making it more difficult to secure a mortgage, which reduces demand even further.

Residential Market

In the residential arena, Realtors consider a balanced market to be one in which homes take an average of six months to sell. This is tracked by calculating the days on market (DOM) for every home listed and sold. If the average DOM rises above six months, then the market is becoming more favorable to buyers. If it falls below that threshold, it is becoming a seller's market. In a buyer's market, there are essentially too many homes for sale for the number of buyers, so inventory increases, homes take longer to sell, and sellers become more motivated and eventually decrease their asking prices.

For example, real estate in Naples, Florida, was considered the most overvalued in the country in 2006. Today, real estate in Naples sells at a 30-plus percent average discount, and the median home price is just $165,500, down from a high of nearly $400,000, according to IHS Global Insight.

Commercial Market

The prevailing consensus amongst commercial real estate investors is that cap rates drive the market. Given the average historical cap rate for a specific asset class (multifamily, retail, office, industrial), properties will be selling below, at, or above the average historical rate. If cap rates are far below the average (as we experienced during the past decade in a compressed cap-rate environment), it's a seller's market. If cap rates are higher than the average, it's a buyer's market. See Table 3.1, which depicts what cap rates need to be for aggressive buying to take place.

Table 3.1 Cap Rates Needed for Aggressive Buying

Based on in-place net operating income (NOI), what do cap rates need to be before you become an aggressive buyer of each of the listed property types and levels?

Property Type	Top-Tier Properties	Mid-Tier Properties	Low-Tier Properties
Apartment	8.2%	9.3%	11.0%
Hotel	10.2%	11.5%	13.6%
Industrial	9.0%	10.2%	12.2%
Mixed use	9.1%	10.0%	11.4%
Office, downtown	9.0%	10.0%	11.6%
Office, suburban	9.6%	10.6%	12.2%
Retail, mall	10.0%	10.8%	12.7%
Retail, grocery/drug-anchored center	9.1%	10.2%	11.7%
Retail, lifestyle/power center	9.6%	10.5%	12.0%
Retail, single tenant	9.3%	10.3%	12.0%

Source: NREI/Marcus & Millichap 2010 Real Estate Investment Outlook

As an example, the national historical average cap rate for multifamily properties is approximately 8 percent. If you're buying at a 12 percent cap rate, it would be considered a buyer's market (assuming that the seller isn't motivated for extraneous reasons). Many first-time buyers needed a significant price correction to be able to afford commercial real estate properties. And experienced investors needed a reset in values in order to justify new acquisitions. Ultimately, investors are more likely to maximize their returns if they are acquiring during a buyer's market and in disposition mode during a seller's market.

4

Distressed Real Estate

Distressed real estate typically refers to property that is in foreclosure or is experiencing some form of financial or physical duress. Distress signifies that the owner of the property or the lender holding the mortgage note is motivated to sell. There is typically no greater opportunity for investors to obtain property at a significant discount to the fair market value.

Obtaining the highest possible price isn't necessarily the goal of a distressed seller. Rather, disposing of the property in a timely manner is of greater importance. Therefore, selling at a price below market value is the norm and not the exception with most distressed situations. The discount obtained in acquiring distressed real estate provides additional equity for the new buyer.

The Present

There are two types of distress:

- *Physically distressed real estate:* The property has a problem and needs to be fixed. Perhaps, it's in poor physical condition or needs capital improvements. For example, the real estate may be run down or dilapidated.

- *Financially distressed real estate:* This refers to the financial condition or state of the property. For example, the owner might not be able to maintain the mortgage payments because the property has been mismanaged, thus resulting in a higher-than-anticipated vacancy rate that fails to generate sufficient income for the owner to meet the monthly debt service. The property could also be in some state of foreclosure or at risk of foreclosure. The lender might agree to a short sale or sell the asset as an REO (real estate owned). The lender might also be willing to sell the note at a discount of the balance owed on the mortgage, and the new buyer would assume responsibility for the foreclosure proceedings to take control of the real estate. Perhaps the owner is distressed because of divorce, death, or poor health. Or, perhaps, the property owner's loan might be maturing and he or she is unable to refinance the existing debt because of a lack of equity.

All these scenarios depict circumstances in which investors have the possibility to acquire real estate at significant discounts. During the new economy, investors are buying properties at bargain-basement prices from owners and lenders who are struggling. The volume of real estate transactions in so-called "distressed" properties will ultimately stabilize the market. But, until then, vulture funds and other savvy investors will continue to circle the skies looking for distressed bargains to prey upon.

RTC Crisis versus the New Economy

Overbuilding and too much supply in the commercial sector were hallmarks of the RTC (Resolution Trust Corporation) and S&L crisis—the last major real estate recession that ended in the early 1990s. However, too much lending and an abundance of easy money in the residential sector caused the current crisis.

There have been nearly endless buying opportunities in the residential sector since the housing collapse in 2007. The bid-ask spread (the difference between what investors were willing to pay and the amount lenders were willing to sell) narrowed in late 2008, and distressed opportunities have become the primary driving force of transactions ever since.

In vast contrast to the residential sector, there has not been as much activity as originally anticipated with distressed commercial assets. Federal regulators have not forced banks to mark to market their bad loans and liquidate their inventory of nonperforming assets. Lenders are savvy to what occurred during the RTC days and want to avoid massive losses. Many lenders prefer to stay the course and sell when the market rebounds. Until the regulators become more forceful, it's unlikely that large-scale deleveraging will occur. That being said, I'm confident we'll ultimately have more deals being consummated on commercial properties (retail, office, industrial, and multifamily). Lenders will eventually realize the cost of extending loans that are underwater and will sell to the highest bidder, especially if the FDIC forces them to do so. Vulture funds have formed to buy all distressed real estate assets, and war chests are being consolidated for a buying spree that many anticipate could last from 2011 through 2013.

Convincing Your Lender

A significant source of real estate bargains will emanate from forced sales by borrowers who have breached banking covenants with their lenders. A breach of covenant results from debt no longer being serviced (mortgages not being paid) by the borrower or the property's value dropping too far below the lender's guidelines.

Many banking representatives have personally admitted to me that a borrower has absolutely no leverage with their lender until he or she defaults on the loan. Assuming that this is accurate, the worst thing a property owner can do is use available cash to keep making interest payments on a property that is worth less than the debt owed on it, especially if the owner has limited cash reserves. Workouts are significantly more effective if the owner has stopped making payments for at least 90 days and the loan has been given to special assets to manage. If the loan officer is still managing your account, it's because the loan is still current. Loans that are current are not problem loans and, thus, typically nonnegotiable.

If you want the lender's attention but can't convince it to consider an extension or short sale of your loan, most borrowers simply stop making payments and then request a meeting with their loan officers to discuss their financial hardship and their proposal to remedy the situation.

Don't burn through your cash reserves if your exit strategy is to hand the keys back to the bank or to broker a short sale on your property. You'll need that cash to pay your ongoing personal expenses and/or to pay attorney fees—assuming you are in litigation with your lender or fighting a deficiency judgment.

Finally, the foreclosing party must produce the note as evidence that he or she is the true owner of the debt. If, for any reason, this evidence cannot be furnished, the lender (or the agent assuming your note) cannot proceed with the foreclosure.

Advantages of Buying a Distressed Property

There are a number of advantages to buying a distressed property:

- A highly motivated seller—either a bank in the case of an REO/foreclosure or owners who are in financial trouble and very interested in getting out of a mortgage they can no longer afford.
- Less emotion from the seller's perspective because the lender considers it a line-item loss to sell for a discount and is interested in getting properties sold and off the liability side of the lender's balance sheet.
- Many foreclosed properties can be purchased for only a percentage of what they would have commanded at the height of the market and at a discount of the current market value.

Disadvantages of Buying a Distressed Property

Disadvantages of buying a distressed property include:

- Although there are bargains to be had, they don't come easily. Great deals are hard won, and there's always competition that can inevitably lead to higher prices.
- There tends to be more legal work required to complete a distressed transaction.
- The time required for short sales or foreclosures often takes longer than traditional transactions.
- Distressed properties can be in tough condition. Owners who know they are going to lose the capital they originally invested are unlikely to maintain the property as they did before, and, in fact, they might even purposely damage it.

The Present

Distressed real estate represents a tremendous opportunity for all investors. Most important, it's an opportunity to acquire real estate assets at steep discounts. And given the record number of foreclosures and the tightening credit market, it will remain a buyer's market for distressed assets for the next several years. Remain optimistic and creative during this cycle. This could be the best time to acquire real estate in our lifetime. Despite what the pundits might say about the demise of real estate and the recession's impact on the industry, opportunities abound, and fortunes will be made as astute investors purchase distressed properties now and either hold them long-term for their cash flow or resell them when the market rebounds.

5

The New Lending Guidelines

There is a new paradigm for financing in this new economy, and it will prevent more homebuyers and investors from qualifying for loans. To put it simply, banks have adopted more stringent guidelines for lending, and obtaining a loan has become significantly more difficult. As an investor, you must fully understand the changes in the financial markets before embarking on any more investments, because financing from here on out is not going to be as easy as it had been in the past.

When a deal is on the line and securing financing is the critical next step, you can't afford to work with inexperienced mortgage brokers or loan officers, because financing in the new economy is no longer a "walk in the park." Working with a local bank and developing a track record of success with the same lender will pay huge dividends for your future business transactions. For instance, when I need to get a deal financed in the Boston area, I work with Peter Hughes of Mt. Washington Bank. He's the consummate professional who understands investors and income-producing properties and doesn't waste time. He'll quickly inform you if financing is available and under what terms it can be provided. I give him all my business because he makes my life easier. You, too, need to find a lender who will be your advocate and partner before and after the loan is made. Repeat business with the same lender will increase the likelihood of your getting deals financed. I'll even pay slightly higher rates with my lender of choice if they come with the security of knowing that my loan application will be processed on time and without delay or surprises.

A good lender will make you aware of the requirements needed to close a deal as well as any obstacles you'll likely encounter. He or she will also thoroughly explain your options without wasting your time. Be very careful in selecting your lenders or mortgage brokers. They are in a position to make or break your deals, so choose very wisely!

9/11 and the Housing Crisis

How well do you remember 9/11? Undoubtedly, you can vividly recall the events of that tragic day, but few of us could have fathomed how this terrorist attack would affect our lives nearly a decade later. Traveling by plane has become much more time-consuming as security screening evolved from a simple procedure we took for granted into a more rigorous investigation. Passengers are required to remove their shoes before passing through metal detectors; carrying liquids greater than 100 milliliters onboard with you has been forbidden; probing questions are posed to suspicious characters; and so on. As the events of 9/11 have had long-lasting effects on how passengers fly commercially, the housing and credit crisis undoubtedly will leave a long-lasting imprint on the way we borrow money.

A few years ago, I realized that financing suddenly had changed when a prospective buyer for one of my buildings spent four months in a failed attempt to secure financing from three lenders. The buyer had a credit score of 750, a wealth of experience owning similar properties, and sufficient and verifiable cash reserves in his bank to account for a 25 percent down payment. In addition the property's existing NOI (net operating income) was more than adequate to service the new level of debt. Nevertheless, these three lenders continually requested documentation from the borrower and delayed the loan commitment for more than 120 days. The buyer was on the verge of giving up before I introduced him to my lender. Needless to say, the closing took place three weeks later (to the satisfaction of all parties), but it wasn't easy—even with an extremely competent lender at the helm. At the closing, however, I realized that financing for future dispositions and acquisitions might never be the same—as I've come to realize that flying commercially would never be the same as it was before 9/11. We eventually realized the importance of going to the airport earlier, wearing loafers instead of shoes with laces, not carrying liquids, and being suspicious of others on our plane. We, too, will adapt to the new lending standards, but it will take time to accept and embrace them as the new reality.

Financing Condos

Condo converters and residential developers should be warned that condos and townhomes pose the greatest challenge for financing these days. Financing guidelines for these kinds of assets have become much stricter, and different rules even apply for new and existing projects. Buyers aren't provided financing for some distressed condos in larger complexes because of the liability associated with the condo reserves.

Assume, for example, that you're a developer of a 20-unit condominium building. The annual condo fees generate $60,000 annually ($3,000 per unit each year). Now, let's assume that you sold 18 units and have two remaining but that 10 of the existing owners are in some state of distress (i.e., foreclosure). If these unit owners stop paying their condo fees, that's a loss of $30,000 to the condo association's reserves that fund the maintenance and upkeep of the property. If the condo association is not able to pay the insurance, make repairs, remove trash, clean the common areas, and so on, then a lender will be hesitant to make a loan on a unit in that property. After all, the condo association might be forced to file for bankruptcy, and most lenders want to avoid these high-risk properties. From a developer's perspective, you'll have a very difficult time selling those two remaining units, and your exposure to lawsuits from existing owners will be exceedingly high.

Detached single-family homes (SFHs) remain the easiest class of property to finance because their historical rates of foreclosure are miniscule when compared to condos, and there's no risk associated with the reserves or lack thereof.

Down Payment

Easy money is no longer available. Good credit, employment history, a significant down payment, and a third-party appraisal are now required. The source of the down payment needs to be documented, and the appraisal needs to justify the purchase price. My lender says that his bank allows borrowers to receive up to 100 percent of the down payment as a monetary gift from family members, but they'll still need to document a saving's history that shows they possess 5 percent of the purchase price to qualify for the loan.

For example:

$500,000—purchase price

$100,000—20 percent down payment required

$100,000—gift from your parents

$ 25,000—you must be able to document that 5 percent of the purchase price exists in your personal accounts

Each lender determines down payment requirements, but the following is a sample of some of the new standards I'm seeing:

- Single-family homes and condos as primary residences typically require a down payment of between 5 and 20 percent.
- FHA loans still require just 3.5 percent down.
- A duplex that will be owner-occupied now requires a minimum of a 20 percent down payment.
- A nonowner-occupied investment property now requires a 25 percent down payment.

Although it's a wonderful time to buy real estate, you must have sufficient capital to make acquisitions given these new financing guidelines. (In actuality, we are just reverting back to the old lending rules.)

Credit Score

Lenders place an enormous amount of importance on FICO scores in determining whether an individual qualifies for a loan. Your credit score provides potential lenders a gauge as to the extent of risk you pose as a borrower. FICO scores range from 300 to 850—the higher the score, the better.

There are three credit-reporting agencies that determine credit-worthiness:

- TransUnion
- Equifax
- Experian

The three agency scores tend to differ because each company calculates FICOs in its own way, and not all creditors report to all three agencies. Credit scores also change frequently over time.

Lenders, therefore, use the middle score to approve a loan and calculate a borrower's interest rate at the time of the application. FICO scores will determine how much one qualifies for as well as the loan terms (interest rate, etc.) lenders will offer.

Every situation and lender are different; however, the lower the loan-to-value (LTV) ratio and the higher the credit score for residential financing, the lower the interest rate tends to be.

A 740 FICO score or higher is typically needed for market interest rates. Unfortunately, I suspect that less than 35 percent of the U.S. population has a FICO score of 740 or higher. If a score is less than 740, one should expect to pay a premium for the loan.

For example, if a lender offers a borrower with a 740 credit score a 5.5 percent interest-rate mortgage, a person with a 540 credit score might be forced to pay 7 percent.

People with good credit, a source of ample current income, and a stable history of paying their bills on time can still secure a loan in the new economy. The length of credit history and the total debt-to-equity ratios also play a factor. Poor credit applicants are being told to pay significantly more for their loans, or they're encouraged to shop elsewhere.

Banks

Between 2000 and 2006, lax lending conditions existed. In fact, it was usually referred to as "easy lending." Lenders lowered underwriting standards and accepted lower credit scores with less verification of income and lower down payments. During this period, many loans were granted even without an appraisal. By early 2007, lending practices began to tighten; however, banks were still making questionable loans through the end of that year.

Some commonly used banking terms during this era included:

- NIV: No income verification
- NAV: No asset verification

The New Lending Guidelines

Banks claim that they are not erecting new hurdles for individual homebuyers and investors seeking loans. But credit problems are not easing. No matter how much additional capital the federal government provides to banks to ease the credit crunch, it appears that they are hoarding the capital or not lending it as easily as they had in the past. Banks will claim, however, that they are not hoarding the capital but that financing standards have changed and fewer people qualify under the new guidelines; therefore, there are fewer loans being made.

The truth of the matter is that banks just aren't ready to ease their newly adopted lending standards because of the severe pain experienced since the collapse of the market. If you had been badly injured from riding a horse, you might think twice about riding again, right? It's no different with banks. They just need some time to forget about the traumatic experiences of the past few years before they can start lending again without fear. After all, most of the banks that survived have lost a lot of money during this crisis and continue to have a significant amount of exposure on their balance sheets. Also, because the secondary market won't buy high-risk loans anymore, lenders won't take on excessive risk because they might actually have to service those loans indefinitely.

There's no such thing as creative lending anymore. Lenders will no longer accept an 80 percent senior loan, 10 percent piggyback or mezzanine, and the remaining balance from some unknown source. Also, nonrecourse loans are hard to find. Lenders are mandating that borrowers claim full responsibility for future payments. The pendulum is swinging to the extremes. It was too easy in 2005 and is becoming too difficult now. If the economy gains traction and the unemployment rate improves, the credit crunch might become less restrictive by 2012. Until then, you must plan for and anticipate a significantly more challenging lending environment.

6

Negotiating with Lenders (Loan Modifications)

I received a phone call one afternoon from a well-spoken gentleman who introduced himself as a friend of a friend. He mentioned that his health-care firm began investing in real estate in 2006 as a way to diversify the company's source of revenue. He then went on to inform me that several of his projects were "under water" and that he had been made aware of my success in negotiating commercial loan modifications on behalf of the investors I worked with.

He requested my assistance in negotiating a loan reduction with his lender. My compensation, if successful, would be a percentage of the savings. The offer: $1 million in cash for a $5 million reduction in the principal of the loan. The lenders eventually countered at 1 for 3, and they actually didn't resist too much. Make no mistake about it; lenders are receptive to modifying loans even if they claim otherwise.

Tishman Speyer Properties has managed a portfolio of assets of more than 116 million square feet consisting of more than 92,000 residential units in major metropolitan areas across the globe. In 2006, Tishman Speyer acquired some very large apartment complexes in New York City for more than $5 billion. The company made those purchases at the high watermark of the speculative bubble market. As rents decreased and the recession deepened, the value of the heavily leveraged real estate dramatically declined. Meanwhile, there were no buyers for these assets, given the overinflated prices. The rental communities weren't able to cover the debt service. Tishman Speyer defaulted on a $3 billion mortgage after an unsuccessful attempt to restructure its debt with senior lenders.

In the winter of 2008, a group of investors hired me to work on a distressed project. The group had purchased an apartment building and adjacent lot with plans to assemble the land and construct a seven–story condominium building. Needless to say, the rental revenue from the apartment building did not justify the purchase price. These investors paid a premium for the asset because they had grander plans for the property. When the market made a turn for the worse, their strategy to develop a larger project on this site never materialized. They were stuck with a property that couldn't sustain itself given the existing debt. Nevertheless, they preferred to remain patient and wait out the market cycle for better days. They wanted me to negotiate a restructuring of their loan. If the debt service could be reduced, the property could sustain itself until conditions improved. They found a private lender willing to provide debt based on the property's existing cash flow. The only problem was that there was a $2 million gap between the new lender's acceptable loan amount and the existing senior note. I began negotiations with the lender to accept a $2 million haircut on their loan if a full payment were made within 15 days. This offer was immediately accepted and the transaction was completed to everyone's satisfaction.

Jorge Pérez is one of the largest condo developers in the country and a billionaire Cuban American real estate entrepreneur. He is known as the Donald Trump of the tropics. After the financial crisis hit in 2007, most of Pérez's projects were in trouble. Ironically, he started a $1 billion vulture fund with the Philadelphia-based private equity firm, Lubert Adler, to buy distressed real estate. Sarcastic comments from local newspapers suggested that he initiated the fund only to buy back his own distressed units.

I'm not an insider at his company, the Related Group, but I know that Mr. Pérez has been vigorously negotiating with his lenders. Along with seeking more time to pay his debt, he is asking bankers to loosen mortgage-lending restrictions so potential buyers of his units can acquire credit to make condo purchases at his properties. When you owe as much as he does (*The Miami Herald* reported more than $2 billion), some would say that Mr. Pérez owns the banks rather than the banks owning him.

Ultimately, the lenders are left with few options. They could extend the loans, sell the debt to investors, or take back the properties. If the lenders ever want to see that $2 billion, they'll extend the loans and work with Pérez until the market rebounds. After all, no one else has the experience and wherewithal to turn that sinking ship around. The banks are far better off forming a partnership with Pérez. Otherwise, they'll need to take a massive haircut on their loans and might lose billions. Though painful at the beginning, a partnership with Pérez will likely mitigate financial losses in the long run.

I guarantee that you are not alone in attempting to restructure a loan with your lender. One-hundred-thousand-dollar condos to multi-billion-dollar portfolios (and everything in between) are being negotiated behind closed doors with lenders across the globe.

The Present

Banks are willing to accept any deal that makes sense to them at the moment. The bank's board of directors makes the final decision regarding offers of this kind, and special assets and/or the loan officers provide guidance to the board. During challenging times like those we're in today, the FDIC is known to apply pressure to the banks' boards to clean up their balance sheets. If you can justify the offer and show duress, the board might accept the deal terms you're offering. Be forewarned that banks don't want to accept a "cram down" on a loan if the borrower has deep pockets and can pay.

Figure out what your options are to refinance and when your loans are set to adjust or mature. Determine your property's current LTV. Maintain your properties because your lenders are less likely to cooperate with you if there's significant deferred maintenance. Reach out to your lenders well before defaulting to warn them of your inability to continue paying. As discussed, you might not have any leverage with them until you default; however, the sooner you start the dialogue, the better chance you'll have of reaching a creative solution. Be sure to emphasize your dire financial situation. It is unlikely that your lender will work with you if you have significant cash reserves. Borrowers must suggest a specific and well-defined plan to their lender. Don't make the mistake of asking your lender how they can modify your loan. It's more than likely that your lender will require more equity to pay down the existing loan and/or request that you have additional reserves. The lender wants to see your financial commitment to the loan. After all, the lender just wants to be paid back in full.

Whether you can no longer continue making loan payments or are already on your fifth month of not paying, contact your loan officer or your lender's special assets department to request a meeting. Offer a way to restructure your loan based on terms that are acceptable to both parties. Deal terms are only limited to your own imagination, so be creative and remain persistent.

Part 3

The Opportunity

7

Reinventing Yourself in the New Economy

Long gone are the days when the perpetual rise of real estate was considered virtually a law of physics. Real estate values could not continue their steep ascent forever. Indeed, the past decade has been a roller-coaster ride that few economists could have anticipated. In fact, most seasoned and highly experienced investors were surprised that the market crumbled so quickly.

Real estate values experienced their most prolific period of appreciation in our nation's history during this past run-up. Virtually every investor made money acquiring, improving, and quickly disposing of real estate assets. Far too many speculators were feverishly buying and selling—and in the process driving up prices. There was a sense of euphoria that enticed the vast majority of investors to shun the time-tested financial models used to value income-producing real estate. Instead, paying a premium was considered logical and appropriate, assuming, of course, that values would continue to soar. Very few investors envisioned a real estate market in decline.

A decade ago, I was acquiring apartment buildings at a fairly decent rate. The business model I subscribed to, however, was not one of random speculation but that of a fairly conservative investor who required his properties to generate an above-average return. Fortunately, I avoided the get-rich-quick schemes that trapped most condo converters at the time—especially those who were late to the game. During the boom most apartment buildings were acquired at numbers that could not support the leverage used to buy them. The owners had to exit quickly by selling the individual units as condos. In other words, the sum of the individual parts was worth more than the entire asset as a whole. But if the market tumbled before exiting, the owner would need to carry a very expensive piece of real estate that could potentially "bleed" him dry.

By 2004, I was acquiring larger apartment complexes using a conservative model based on simple rental economics. But, by early 2005, I had made a personal (and quite fortuitous) decision to relocate to a warmer climate. That year Boston was pummeled by several blizzards, and we Bostonians endured blistering temperatures. I had also been working nonstop for the past 15 years and needed a break.

The idea was simple: Cash out of what I owned and take a year off to reevaluate my situation. Thaw out for a few months in southern Florida and—when rested and relaxed—attempt to duplicate the success I had experienced in the North in my new locale.

In the spring of 2005, many speculators had expressed interest in buying my properties. Of course, they wanted to convert my apartment buildings to condos. Conversion had been an extremely profitable endeavor up to that point, so the market was ripe to sell during that severely compressed, cap-rate environment. I had originally purchased buildings at no lower than a 9 percent cap rate and was receiving offers in the 3 to 4 percent range. I simply couldn't justify holding the properties when I ran the numbers and considered the associated risks and rewards.

Reinventing Yourself in the New Economy

Admittedly, I did not possess an all-knowing crystal ball that warned me of the market's pending doom. In reality, the guiding principle that helped me make the decision to liquidate at that point was actually advice my father once imparted to me when I was much younger: "Son, you'll never lose money if you sell for a profit."

In other words, one should never be too greedy. It was rather rudimentary advice coming from a physician, not a real estate mogul. But it was practical advice that certainly resonated with me at the time. I told myself to get out while the getting was still good. I bought at X and sold for a significantly higher price. My initial plan was to take the money off the table and eventually divert it to another market where I could hopefully duplicate my success.

What I hadn't fully realized at the time was that you shouldn't buy property in a market that you don't intimately understand. Now I repeatedly warn my readers to stay within their farm areas. It's a message that is found in all of my books. After all, it takes a minimum of a few years to become well acquainted with a new area.

I spent three years in the southern Florida market touring real estate assets and analyzing the numbers on each property. After viewing nearly 200 properties, I realized that the compressed cap-rate environment was even worse in Florida than it was in New England. Properties traded regularly at 2 to 3 percent caps. I refused to overpay like one of those speculators who bought my properties at sub 5 percent caps in Boston just a few years earlier. It just didn't feel right, so I opted to trust my instincts and wait. Because I couldn't find properties that would provide a positive cash flow based on their existing numbers (I never use pro forma estimates), I avoided any new acquisitions for several years.

I recall meeting with the sales director at a widely known, national brokerage firm in Miami. He told me not to expect to do business in Florida if one of my acquisition parameters was that the property generate a positive cash flow based on its current rental income and a 25 percent down payment. For a guy who thrived on doing deals, I was rather dealless from 2006 through 2009.

During that period, however, I delved into my new market and met all the important players. I took time to understand each street, neighborhood, and town at a more granular level.

What I soon realized was that I'd need to reinvent myself if I wanted to actively remain working in real estate. I wasn't a speculative condo converter and certainly wasn't going to buy properties at such low cap rates. I was prudent enough to avoid risky investments that couldn't produce a large enough NOI to service the property's debt.

Reengineering your business plan and diversifying your emphasis to recession-proof sectors is critical. In recessionary times, you sometimes must consider departing from an existing business plan, even if it led to great success in the past.

Most successful entrepreneurs realize that reinventing themselves and their businesses is a healthy process that can pay huge dividends if executed properly. If what you had been doing in the past no longer works, you need to change gears, develop a new way of thinking, and change your business model to meet the demands of a new environment.

Because I couldn't buy income-producing real estate, I decided to concentrate on building a transaction-based business based on what I envisioned as a future opportunity—a distressed real estate market that would eventually present tremendous buying opportunities.

I figured that 2 to 3 percent cap rates couldn't be sustained forever. Admittedly, I now had the advantage of being familiar with the Boston, Midwest, and southern Florida markets. No matter how spectacular the run-up in prices seemed to have gotten in Boston, it couldn't compare to what I was seeing in Miami. I realized that a tremendous opportunity existed, but I needed to act swiftly.

I began meeting with developers who wouldn't complete their projects for another 12 to 24 months. I introduced myself to attorneys who specialized in bankruptcy law. I also met with loan officers at most local community banks in my farm area. Because there wasn't a flood of loan defaults in early 2006, most lenders hadn't yet established a loss mitigation or special assets department (a division within a bank that mitigates the losses for the lender). I spent 2006 and 2007 investing my time in what I perceived as a future opportunity. There were no guarantees, of course, that my new dedication would ultimately lead to a viable new business, but by 2008 it was clear that my time had been well spent.

My company's emphasis during the boom years changed from taking equity positions on income-producing real estate to brokering institutional multifamily deals and launching a retail-oriented brokerage firm. Both business lines were transaction-based and kept me in the game and well-informed until I felt the market was ripe to reenter—which is the case in 2011.

In fact, my first significant project was a large apartment complex that the developers failed to convert. I was the first person to introduce the troubled asset to the lenders—informing them of the project and its imminent demise. The loan was still performing at the time (i.e., the borrowers were still making payments), so the loss mitigation department had not flagged the account. Fortunately, however, I was first in line to attempt a purchase of the note. There was a "seasoning" period of about six months (three months from the time the developer stops making payments plus another three months for the manager of the loss mitigation department to consider all his options) before the lender is willing to consider a discounted note sale, but I was well-positioned to match a buyer with the lender, at a price that would work for both parties.

Our retail business was somewhat similar to our multifamily business. Compressed cap rates in the multifamily sector made it challenging to continue buying. The numbers just didn't pencil out, so we developed a business that would benefit from the downturn in the market before it occurred. Our ventures in retail started because of our desire to acquire shopping centers. Unfortunately, we were not as familiar as we wanted to be with the southern Florida retail market to make prudent deci-sions regarding potential acquisitions. To gain the experience needed, we started a retail brokerage firm that represented both tenants and landlords (i.e., tenant rep and landlord rep). In other words, we helped retailers expand by finding new retail locations and assisted retail property owners lease their vacant space. In less then three years, we developed a marvelously successful retail brokerage firm that now represents more than 200 locations.

Through sheer determination and perseverance, I was able to create two new profit centers that would thrive during the recession. What I had been doing with a great deal of success in the past (buying value-add apartment buildings, renovating them, renting them at a premium, and generating a positive income stream and a healthy return on my initial investment) clearly was not working by 2006. The compressed cap-rate environment caused by condo converters made it impossible to generate a decent return on rental buildings. I couldn't have grown my business had I been adamant about staying the course. In fact, I probably avoided a financial disaster by not buying during those overinflated years. Fortunately, I had a sense of how the changes in the industry would affect my business and decided to adjust my business during the downturn.

Case Study

Miguel Solis of Prudential Florida Realty is a residential real estate broker. He had done quite well for himself during the boom years, but he quickly realized (after barely surviving a financially disastrous 2007) that he needed to change his business model. He was determined to survive the downturn and realized that the market's appetite for real estate speculation had gone from boom to bust. Also, he under-stood the importance of changing his model to prosper in a depleted real estate economy.

Reinventing Yourself in the New Economy

He immediately stopped trying to sell preconstruction condominiums and started a vigorous campaign to partner with lender-processing service companies. These firms provide automated loan processing, risk management, and other support services that complete the process from loan boarding to payoff. He realized that these service providers were the banks' gatekeepers in liquidating distressed properties. If he could find a way to partner with these companies, he would position himself as the "go-to" broker for moving a significant amount of real estate at discounted prices. And sales of distressed real estate, in his opinion, were where the future opportunity existed. He would change his model of selling fewer properties at high prices to selling significantly more properties at discounted prices. Miguel explained the boom years as days filled by writing up offers and sending them out to property owners. His buyers would typically bid more than the asking price on all of his transactions. There were very few listings available, so he concentrated on the buy side. He closed 17 deals with 1 client in November 2005! His buyers would acquire and then flip, so he had multiple transactions with each client. During the apex of the euphoria (2004 to 2005), one of his clients earned a net profit of approximately $3.5 million on more than 100 transactions.

Miguel said, "My savvy clients started dumping everything in early 2006. They wanted out immediately." By the first quarter of 2007, the market had completely changed. His customers were inquiring about short sales, so he bought every book on the subject and attended distressed real estate seminars in an effort to learn as much as possible.

He called local bank representatives every day for four months before he received his first REO listing. By late 2007, he was doing 7 to 10 short sales a month and was 100 percent dedicated to distressed real estate. He even expanded his services to help banks maintain their properties until they could be sold. He hired cleanup crews, locksmiths, maintenance personnel, and other specialists to help banks with their new real estate responsibilities.

The Opportunity

Miguel now claims that he works harder than ever before, but the money is still very good. The year 2010 was extremely busy. He was inundated with calls from buyers wanting to acquire distressed real estate. All his transactions are short sales. Thankfully, the banks are finally cooperating.

He says that he expects short sales to remain his "bread and butter" business through 2011 and 2012. In fact, a typical month in 2010 yielded 17 transactions, and he's just as busy now as he was during the boom—he earned a high six-figure income in 2010.

A friend of mine is a real estate attorney for a well-respected law firm in Florida. At one time, he primarily worked on closings and had an extremely busy practice until 2006. When the number of closings started to slide, he realized that it was time to change the way he did business. Otherwise, he wouldn't have survived for much longer.

He came to the conclusion that the deep market fissures in the housing market would last for several more years, so he convinced his law firm to reposition him as the head legal counsel for its REO department. I'm glad to report that, as of late 2010, he was closing on average 90 to 100 deals each month and making three times his previous salary.

I've worked quite closely in the past with executives of The Laramar Group, a Chicago-based private equity group. They found it extremely difficult to buy any new properties in 2008, so they created a new receivership division in early 2009 to capitalize on the distressed market. Today, that division manages more than 4,000 units at 51 properties across 7 states, and this new business division is highly profitable.

The moral of the story is that you shouldn't expect the same spectacular results every year if you don't consider modifying your business strategy to adapt to the changing times. Whatever you had been doing from 2000 through 2007 will likely no longer work. This is a *new* economy, and the sooner you realize it the better off you'll be. The only way to achieve long-term success in real estate (or any other industry, for that matter) is to embrace a periodic reinvention and/or modification of what you do and how you do it and to accept change as necessary to your survival. You must determine where the new opportunities exist and how to leverage your skills and expertise to take your piece of the distressed American pie. It's time to sink or swim—to flounder or flourish. Welcome to the new economy.

8

The Gold Rush of 1849

The American dream depicts industrious young Puritans working diligently year after year. They were content to slowly accumulate modest fortunes over a lifetime of hard work. In fact, Benjamin Franklin often wrote about the honor of the Puritan work ethic, good values, hard work, and character in his *Poor Richard's Almanac*: "A penny saved is a penny earned."

The American dream, however, was suddenly shattered in 1849 with the discovery of gold in California. Significant wealth creation—earned virtually overnight by sheer will, determination, and a fair amount of good luck in the gold mines of northern California—ruled the day. Instant gratification became the new mantra in America.

Does the notion of getting rich quickly sound familiar? The Internet entrepreneurs of the 1990s likely had much in common with the 49ers of the mid-nineteenth century.

The Opportunity

When gold was discovered in northern California, millions of Americans, Europeans, and Asians immediately migrated to the area. San Francisco became the geographical focal point for anyone who aspired to overnight fame and fortune. The city quickly grew and soon became a rival of New York in terms of wealth, prestige, and commerce. A small number of prospectors who searched for gold in California's rivers and mines found the fortune they were hoping for. Unfortunately, however, the vast majority of the 49ers left California as poor (if not poorer) as when they had arrived. By vast contrast, significantly more fortunes were made from entrepreneurs who provided goods and services to the millions of miners and other migrants who had relocated to the area.

Merchants, in fact, made more than miners during and after the gold rush of 1849. Allow me to repeat myself: "Merchants made more money than miners during and after the gold rush of 1849." The profundity of this statement and how it applies to you requires further explanation.

As stated, a few early gold seekers did make a modest profit. Most, however, especially those arriving late to California, didn't find gold and made little to nothing.

Other businesspeople, through good fortune and hard work, reaped great fortunes in retail, entertainment, lodging, and transportation. In other words, fortunes were made in sectors that had nothing to do with gold but everything to do with savvy entrepreneurs who realized a good business opportunity and seized the moment. Many service-oriented businesses were highly profitable because of the influx of people to northern California. After all, the gold seekers left everything behind from where they came but needed to sustain themselves while they were in California.

According to historical records, the wealthiest man in California during the early years of the gold rush was Samuel Brannan. He was a successful shopkeeper who opened the first supply stores near the gold fields in northern California. He supplied the earlier fortune seekers with basic provisions and made a fortune doing it.

The Gold Rush of 1849

Levi Strauss was another such fortune maker with great vision and an eye for future opportunities. Arriving in California in the 1850s, Strauss opened a dry goods wholesale business. Strauss sold a variety of goods to the supply stores throughout California. However, one product eventually became one of the most enduring fixtures in American culture: Levi's jeans. Levi Strauss initially introduced the durable pants to miners in the gold mines, but they remained popular long after the gold rush ended. In fact, more than 150 years later, Levi Strauss & Co. has become one of the largest apparel marketers in the world with sales in more than 100 countries.

OK (big, deep breath), how is this relevant to you and real estate investing in the new economy? Well, there have been many booms and busts during recorded history:

- In the 1630s, the tulip bulb mania in Holland was followed by a sudden collapse in prices. This was thought to be the first speculative bubble in recorded history.

- In the 1840s and 1850s, the California gold rush (as previously discussed) was followed by a tumultuous economic collapse in northern California that transformed once-prosperous mining towns into ghost towns.

- The Roaring '20s were followed by the Great Depression and the collapse of the stock market that started in 1929.

- In the late 1990s, the dot-com bubble was followed by the Internet implosion.

- And by the early twenty-first century, the boom in U.S. real estate was followed by the subprime mortgage crisis, global economic meltdown, and the Great Recession.

I have been an active participant, beneficiary, and avid student of the past two bubbles. But I think it would be helpful to reflect on the successes of the 1840s to better understand how some entrepreneurs developed unique and highly profitable businesses in a changing market.

Common everyday items were in short supply during the gold rush. Shortly after Levi Strauss's arrival in San Francisco, he began selling canvas to use for tents. Soon he realized that prospectors needed pants that were sufficiently durable to withstand the hard physical labor required from individuals who toiled in the mines all day long. Strauss decided to convert the canvas to overalls for the miners. When the gold rush ended, Strauss didn't close up shop. Instead, he modified the miner's overalls into blue jeans—a product that became wildly popular to a much larger market.

When Levi Strauss migrated from New York to San Francisco, he knew that his fortune wouldn't be made in the gold mines. In other words, he didn't follow the herd. Instead, he remained dedicated to supplying miners with everyday products that they needed. Levi Strauss made his great fortune after the gold rush had subsided by selling millions of his trademark blue jeans to miners and nonminers alike. By altering his product, he was able to broaden his customer base. That's a priceless lesson for today's economy.

Fortunes Made in Ancillary Businesses

Following the masses in their pursuit of great fortune doesn't always result in the most profitable outcome. During the gold rush, the most obvious decision made by wealth seekers was to search for gold. During the Internet boom, investors bought tech stocks or developed Internet companies. During the real estate boom, they acquired properties. More often than not, however, the business models that lead to the real pot of gold are not so obvious. People with great ingenuity and creativity often develop the very best moneymaking ideas. After all, Levi Strauss didn't pursue the most obvious path (at that time) to great wealth. He wasn't a gold seeker. Rather, he offered a unique product that was widely adopted even after the frenzy subsided.

Lawyers are now making a fortune conducting closings for short sale transactions. Bankruptcy specialists are experiencing an unprecedented boom in this Great Recession. Receivers are turning a very nice profit managing distressed properties during these tough times. Real estate brokers who specialize in foreclosed real estate are doing extremely well during the busted economy. There are a host of entrepreneurs who now service the distressed real estate sector and are more profitable now than they were during the run-up in real estate values.

Modifying Your Strategy after the Boom

Successful business owners must have the foresight to change gears before, during, and after a boom in order to make and/or sustain their fortune. Opportunities abound, regardless of the times. An excellent example of this comes from a friend of mine who founded a business to connect "bottom-fishing" real estate investors with distressed condo deals. Peter Zalewski and his wife had dinner at my house a few years ago. At the time, he had recently launched CondoVultures.com, a fore-closure real estate brokerage firm that only represented buyers, but his business was still in its infant stages of development and still hadn't evolved into a serious profit center. My wife and I recall that Peter had a passion for what he did and was a guy who had an innate ability to explain complex matters in memorable, short sound bites.

Peter was betting on the real estate market collapse and was creating his business model during the boom to become the preferred brokerage firm for investors searching for bargains during the pending bust. Before becoming the Condo King of Miami, however, he was a journalist at the *Miami Herald*. He, therefore, understood what it took to obtain "ink" (i.e., free PR) in publications. He understood the power of the media and created a proprietary database of information about the southern Florida condo market and disseminated his coveted information for free to the press. His database consisted of all condos in southern Florida that had been on the market for no less then 100 days and had been reduced in price by at least 100,000. He became such a revered expert in the field that he appeared in Michael Moore's documentary, *Capitalism, A Love Story*. He also appeared in *Time* magazine and on *60 Minutes*. "We are here to help buyers capitalize on the condo correction. In times of distress and in times of downturn, there's opportunity," Zalewski often said. Within a few years, his firm grew from 2 people to almost 40. Ever since the Great Recession began, he has been wildly successful selling millions of dollars' worth of distressed condos throughout Florida.

Another friend of mine made a fortune pumping concrete. He was not interested in buying real estate. Instead, he discovered a niche market to exploit during the boom. He provided his services to developers of skyscrapers who needed cement pumped to hard-to-reach job sites (i.e., to the thirtieth, fortieth, or fiftieth floors of high-rise development projects). He charged a premium and earned a fortune because there was little competition for this particular service. But when the boom years ended and construction dried up, he began to explore the possibility of providing his services to countries such as China and Brazil—regions of the world that were economically strong and still very much under construction. Much like Levi Strauss, he seized upon a good business idea but modified it to meet the changing times.

Another acquaintance of mine was a developer from Argentina. In 1998, he was assembling plots of land on Miami's Biscayne Bay for a development project. He secured entitlements and permits to construct a 50-story condominium building. Two years later, he sold both the plans and the fully entitled land to a developer and earned more than a 20 million payday! He took those earnings and allocated them to another high-rise project of his own. Unfortunately, he couldn't finish the building before the bust and eventually lost everything when his lender foreclosed on the property. However, he didn't quit or give up after this tragic event. He decided to reinvent himself and his business. By leveraging his banking contacts and ability to source distressed real estate, he is now brokering multimillion deals for several investment groups from Latin America. He finds distressed projects, conducts the due diligence, assembles the investment team, and manages the property back to health. His investors supply the capital needed to acquire the assets, and he earns a 25 percent equity stake for each deal. He also serves as the general partner in charge of the day-to-day operations. If you get knocked down, you must find a way to get back up.

Ideas for viable businesses during challenging economic times aren't always so obvious. Sometimes you'll stumble upon a good concept, and other times you'll methodically develop one out of necessity. Always remember that there are just as many, if not more, profitable opportunities to pursue during the doom-and-gloom years associated with a bust as there are during the go-go days associated with the boom. If you were successful during the boom, then you can be equally successful during the bust. The gold rush gave Levi Strauss his big opportunity, but the period following that boom gave him his fortune. Pay close attention to your ever-changing business environment and be willing to adopt new strategies to profit in the downturn.

9

Transaction-Based Real Estate Businesses

As discussed in earlier chapters, I couldn't find any properties to buy at my desired cap rate in Miami during the boom. Instead of grinding it out and refusing to work until the market conditions changed in my favor, I decided to modify the way I did business. Instead of having an equity position in real estate assets (i.e., ownership in properties), I created a commercial brokerage firm that represented shopping center owners and retailers and matched lenders with investors of distressed apartment buildings investors who were prepared to buy early in the cycle). These sorts of businesses helped to diversify my company's revenue stream, provided the chance to develop an expertise in the local market, and afforded me the opportunity to earn very lucrative brokerage fees.

The Opportunity

I began by representing several local retailers throughout southern Florida. One deal with a national chain led to representation for a landlord at another property. That landlord representation led to more tenant rep opportunities. Consequently, the multiplier effect took hold, and I found myself actively representing retailers throughout the region. With hard work, determination, and perseverance, I developed the fledgling commercial brokerage business into a very healthy profit center; one that would position me to assume equity positions in local deals.

As with most professional endeavors, the most important factor in generating new business is to remain honest and ethical during all your business transactions. Everything else tends to take care of itself. Protecting your reputation and being known for your professionalism, business acumen, and competence will eventually pay huge dividends.

I know a very astute investor from Boston who was buying apartment complexes a decade ago throughout that city. Eventually, he launched a real estate brokerage firm and located it in one of his mixed-use buildings. After a few years, he had about 20 sales associates working for him and founded a property management team. He basically had a lock on his farm area because the majority of the local sales and rentals went through his firm. Here's how:

- He would cherry-pick the best deals to buy before they made it to the general market.
- He would always show his apartments (before showing units from other owners) to prospective tenants who called his office inquiring about vacancies.
- He used market intelligence that he gathered from his active team of brokers to get ahead of the curve on almost everything that would affect his business.

In sum, this shrewd entrepreneur had a self-made competitive advantage over everyone else.

Transaction-Based Real Estate Businesses

The other transaction-based business I started matches investors with distressed multifamily assets. Inasmuch as I had very good banking contacts, I was able to access the nonperforming loans lists from several distressed lenders. Of course, they wanted to remove these toxic assets from their balance sheets, so it was a question of matching distressed real estate opportunities with investor capital and taking my share of the equity.

One of my good friends from the Midwest owns more than 3,000 apartment units and nearly half a million square feet of retail and office space. According to him, the market had been slow for new transactions during the past few years, so he developed a new side business that has compensated him extremely well during the past 12 months. "Matt: I've bought and sold 45 mortgages in the past 11 months for a net profit of $1.4 million."

During one of my discussions with an investor in the medical area, I was told that a broker named Ken Weston was the medical condo king of Miami. That same day, I Googled his name and learned that he was, in fact, a very successful medical real estate broker, developer, and consultant. In fact, his firm has handled more than 13 million square feet of commercial condominium space, and he has sold more than 3 billion in medical real estate.

I worked with Ken on a project and had the privilege to become better acquainted with him. In 2007, he noticed that the market to sell medical office space was waning. He changed gears immediately and concentrated on leasing space to doctors. He informed me that his brokerage business now represents more than 50 percent of his company's annual revenue. He's still an equity player on deals, but the buildings he buys require 3 to 10 years to develop and sell. The brokerage business, however, provides steady and consistent cash flow year after year.

The primary advantage of owning an active brokerage business or working as a transactional broker is that it can serve as a major cash cow that pays your monthly expenses. Brokerage businesses tend to have modest overhead but can produce a significant amount of cash flow. Unlike equity plays, the brokerage business doesn't require your own investment capital when you're working on a deal. You can earn commissions upward of 6 percent (or more) of the transaction price. In fact, you can sometimes forfeit your commission and trade it for an equity position in the deal. If you want to maintain a good pulse on the market and be involved in deal flow, I highly recommend being in the real estate brokerage business.

Case Study

Paco Diaz is the senior vice president of retail properties at CB Richard Ellis (CBRE). He is known as "the big box king" of Miami. He leases the largest retail spaces in town and has been doing it successfully since 1983.

During the boom era, he was extremely active, and his deals were closing rapidly. Land was moving quickly, and retailers were opening stores at a fairly good rate. Projects that were dormant for years suddenly came alive again. In fact, 2005 was the very best year in his illustrious career. "I couldn't do anything wrong," said Paco. That year, he sold a very large parcel of land to a national shopping center developer and sold several other large projects. He was ranked the No. 1 retail broker for CBRE nationwide. Paco admits that "hard work, local knowledge of the market, a laser-sharp customer focus, and a bit of good luck" made him successful.

However, good times always come to an end. In mid-2008, it all changed. Banks stopped lending; retailers stopped expanding; developers stopped buying land; vacancy rates in shopping centers lingered. Paco's listings—which just a year before received multiple offers—now received very few offers. "It seems like it occurred almost overnight," Paco said.

He continues to represent both retailers and landlords—working both sides of the equation. He is still oriented toward the bigger deals rather than smaller ones. He works harder and smarter than before, and deals take longer to get done. Paco says he just doesn't have the luxury to waste time, so he's highly selective about how he dedicates his time during his workweek.

He predicts that the market will start improving by mid-2011, when banks begin lending again and employers start hiring. According to Paco, the future will look like this:

- Lots of cash on the sidelines waiting to buy.
- Banks will have to bite the bullet and sell properties.
- Owners will sell at a discount.
- Higher prices will follow when the economy improves.
- Every property is different—so location is critical.
- C and B– properties must offer big concessions and lower rents to attract tenants.
- Grade A properties will be in much better shape to ride out the downturn.
- In fact, rents will continue to increase in A locations.
- The low end retailers will remain very healthy. Subway, Dollar Stores, T.J. Maxx, and so on are all making money.
- There are no new locations to move into because there's no new development.

His last words of sage advice: "Take good care of your clients throughout the downturn, and you'll do well when the economy recovers."

10

Commercial Real Estate

During the past four years, I've been waiting patiently for the collapse of the commercial real estate sector (in particular, retail and multifamily) so that I could start buying again. A quick study of previous real estate cycles shows that a downturn in the commercial sector historically follows the unraveling of the residential market. In fact, most real estate experts agree that commercial real estate is the next shoe to drop in this ever-changing world of ours.

In early 2010, a Congressional oversight panel for the Troubled Asset Relief Program (TARP) stated (on record) its opinion about the future of the banking system as it relates to commercial real estate:

> Over the next few years, a wave of commercial real estate loan failures could threaten America's already-weakened financial system. Commercial loan losses could jeopardize the stability

of many banks, and as the damage spreads beyond individual banks, it will contribute to prolonged weakness throughout the economy.

With commercial property values declining by nearly 40 percent since 2007 (resulting from higher vacancy rates, lower rents, and increasing concessions), it is estimated that about 50 percent of all commercial real estate loans will be under water by the end of 2010. Making matters even worse, $1.4 trillion in commercial real estate loans will mature in the next four years, and many of the borrowers won't be able to refinance into fixed long-term loans.

The Retail Sector

The adage in retail real estate is that, "Retail follows rooftops." Shopping center developers tend to follow residential builders. As single-family homes, condominiums, and townhouses are constructed and people move into their new dwellings, shopping center developers follow soon thereafter. But rest assured that, when rooftops dwindle, retail is not far behind. Retail has always been largely dependent on residential real estate as its engine and primary source of growth. I prefer infill retail projects near established residential, office, and industrial projects—in proximity to the places where people live and work.

As unemployment increases, consumer confidence dwindles, and families begin losing their homes to foreclosure, the demand for retail space declines. Think about it this way: If you fear losing your job because everyone around you is being laid off, aren't you going to reduce the number of times you eat out at expensive restaurants, get your haircut at the salon, and buy new clothes at your favorite shop? During lean times, everyone cuts back on unnecessary expenses. Individuals will dine at home more often and avoid eating out. They might launder their own clothes versus dry-cleaning them, and, perhaps, they'll extend the time between visits to the hair salon. They will delay or cancel the purchase of a new plasma TV or washer/dryer. As consumers reduce their discretionary spending, retailers feel the direct impact to their bottom lines. Retail sales decline because consumers won't spend as much as they had in the past. Eventually, retailers aren't able to keep up with their expenses, and they close shop. The same holds true for the office sector. Do you think the local accountant, physician, attorney, or other professional will expand his or her office or lease additional space while such economic uncertainty looms overhead? Do you think large corporations will expand their operations to other cities if their sales are sliding and they are forecasting lower revenues?

The depressed economy has created a rise in commercial vacancies that has affected property owners' ability to maximize net operating income (NOI). The owners of retail and office assets find themselves at the mercy of the existing tenants because of the fallout. Many tenants who managed to survive during the downturn are requesting rent abatements (a reduction in rent for a specified period) to weather the storm. It's a vicious cycle in which overleveraged investors find themselves under a great deal of duress—especially the commercial property owners who made acquisitions at the peak of the market.

Lower property values result from higher vacancy rates, lower rents, and the subsequent drop in a property's NOI. Investors who purchased a commercial property in 2002 to 2008 likely wished they hadn't. Their properties are probably worth less than what they paid for them. Moreover, they're unable to refinance their mortgages without making a significant capital contribution to pay down the existing debt and achieve an acceptable loan-to-value ratio.

A commercial real estate crisis will wreak havoc from 2010 through 2014, as commercial mortgages come due for refinancing on projects that are under water. Risk-adverse lenders aren't willing to refinance existing debt unless the ratios are in line with the lending standards established by the new economy. These conditions are taking a heavy toll on owners of apartment, retail, office, and industrial buildings. The new economy—with its constricted credit markets—has made it impossible for many property owners to refinance their loans.

Here's an example. Let's assume that in 2006 you acquired a large shopping center for $100 million. You bought the property with 20 percent down (or $20 million), so your principal mortgage balance is $80 million.

The property performed well until 2008. That year, however, brought new challenges that you hadn't anticipated. For example, you began to notice red flags that included new leases being signed at a 20 percent discount compared to leases signed for similar space just 12 months ago. Vacancy rates increased as you lost tenants to the souring economy. Existing tenants requested a reduction in their rents, and you were obliged to give it to them to keep them in place. New prospective tenants demanded significantly more tenant improvement allowances (TIAs) than what you had offered to any other tenants since acquiring the property.

By late 2008, you're barely breaking even with all the financial obligations associated with the property. The loan on the property will mature in 2011, and you owe more on the property than it's currently worth. Let's assume that the property is now worth $60 million based on the most recent appraisal, but you still owe $80 million. Your equity (that $20 million you deposited on closing day) has disappeared suddenly, and you don't qualify for refinancing because your lender has adopted tighter lending standards and will accept only a 75 percent LTV on the currently appraised value. You quickly do the math and realize that the bank will offer you only a $45 million loan. To refinance, you'll need to make up the difference—a whopping $35 million in cash.

You're wondering whether you should make the next mortgage payment once you realize that the possibility for your situation to improve is rather bleak. You become less motivated to continue making payments on a property that's only worth $60 million. (Don't forget, you owe $80 million!) You'll soon be bleeding money, and you certainly don't have an extra $35 million sitting in your bank account for the refinancing. When the loan matures (assuming you make it that far), you'll be faced with two options:

- Come up with the $35 million to refinance.
- Give the property's keys back to the lender.

This scenario is by no means far-fetched; it will be a nightmare repeated for many property owners throughout the country. Thousands of commercial property owners will find themselves in financial dire straits in the next four years. In fact, total commercial real estate losses are estimated to exceed $300 billion.

The chief economist from CB, Richard Ellis, recently made the following comment to the *New York Times*: "Anyone who purchased (commercial) property in the past six years has their equity pretty well washed out." (Charles V. Bagli, "Buying Landmarks? Easy. Keeping Them? Maybe Not," *New York Times*, January 16, 2010). As I'm writing this chapter, I find myself in the midst of negotiating a deal for the acquisition of a $70 million shopping center from an extremely distressed developer. We've been waiting on the sidelines for many years now, and it's finally time to get back into the market. In fact, this developer was one of the largest acquirers of retail real estate during the past seven years. The problem is that he started buying in 2002 and used short-term debt to finance his real estate. The firm acquired a dozen or so projects totaling several million square feet of retail real estate. Unlike residential mortgages with 30-year terms, commercial mortgages often run between 3 and 10 years. It's relatively short-term debt because most developers buy vacant land (or acquire existing properties), entitle the land, secure permits, develop, lease (or renovate), reposition the property, maximize the NOI, stabilize the asset, and sell to the highest bidder. That's their value-add cycle. Perhaps the developer will even secure a construction loan with the expectation that he'll be able to refinance into long-term debt once he stabilizes the property. Three to ten years is a reasonable amount of time to achieve those goals because it typically takes less time to fully execute a plan and exit given, of course, a predictable market cycle. In this example, the developer began making acquisitions in 2002, and most of his loans will mature in 2011 and 2012.

What to Expect

Since building values have declined so much and lending standards have become incredibly more stringent, disposition of properties for at least the balance of the outstanding loan is, in many cases, not a viable option. Furthermore, refinancing is no longer an option either. Developers can't sell their properties for what it cost them to build, so many are exploring the possibility of negotiating a short sale with their lenders to get out from under the exorbitant debt that they can't possibly repay. Others are attempting to convince their lenders to extend their loans with the hope that the market eventually will rebound in their favor.

The problem is expected to mount as more loans mature and as the economy continues to languish. After all, no one expected nearly 50 percent declines in property values and the worst recession since 1929. I would argue that the short-term implications for the commercial real estate industry are alarming and that many property owners (particularly those who paid a premium during the past few years and financed their acquisitions with short-term debt) ultimately will lose their properties to foreclosure.

Most industry experts estimate that commercial loan delinquencies will peak in 2012. In the meantime, lenders may deal with the problem by reworking the troubled loans or extending their maturity dates. The primary advantage for banks to extend loans is that they don't have to "mark to market" assets on their balance sheets. (Mark to market refers to the assignment of the current market price to assets on their books while recognizing the loss.) Most lenders prefer to avoid foreclosure because they aren't in the business of property ownership nor do they want to alarm the FDIC, so they might try to extend the maturity date of their troubled loans to give the borrower more time to figure out a solution. The industry refers to this activity as "extend and pretend" because the lenders extend the loan and pretend that they won't have to take a loss on it.

Lenders will consider extending the term of a loan to avoid writing down the value of the asset—that could be as high as 50 percent. Eventually, however, the FDIC will force lenders to clean up their books and take losses by selling their nonperforming loans or owned inventory of real estate to investors at steep discounts. Once the federal regulators and/or lenders decide that loan extensions are no longer working, the floodgates should open and investment opportunities will likely abound for the patient capital that's been sitting on the sidelines waiting for the commercial market to hit bottom. But until both lenders and owners accept the new valuations on their properties and sell at existing market prices, a large-scale recovery is unlikely to occur.

11

Retail Real Estate

Retail real estate includes shopping centers, strip malls, outlet centers, and so on. The usual suspects to lease retail space include national tenants such as AT&T, GameStop, Starbucks, McDonald's, Wendy's, Great Clips, Auto Zone, 7-Eleven, The Vitamin Shoppe, Chipotle, and large, big-box, national retail tenants (often referred to as anchor tenants) such as BJ's, Home Depot, Target, Best Buy, OfficeMax, Staples, Michaels, Toys "R" Us, and the granddaddy of them all—Walmart!

Retail tenants are categorized into the following three groups: national chains, such as Subway, that has more than 31,000 locations worldwide; regional concepts, such as Upper Crust Pizzeria with 20 locations in the Boston area; or "mom-and-pop" businesses such as Ted's Dry Cleaning company that may service a local community with only one store.

The 10 largest franchise systems in the United States are:

1. Subway (22,227 locations nationally)
2. McDonald's (12,127)

3. Jani-King (9,713)

4. Curves (7,091)

5. Burger King (6,343)

6. Jazzercise (6,280)

7. Ameriprise Financial (5,853)

8. Jackson Hewitt (5,610)

9. Dunkin' Donuts (5,213)

10. Pizza Hut (5,084)

As reported by FRANdata, the fastest-growing new franchises include:

1. HealthSource

2. Instant Tax Service

3. SuperSlow Zone

4. Auction It TODAY

5. Premier Rental-Purchase

6. Math Monkey

7. Guard-A-Kid

8. World Properties International

9. Cellairis

10. DNA Services of America

Retail Demand

The need for retail property in a given area is dependent on the local household demand for goods and services. The aggregate demand for retail space nationally is dependent on specific consumption patterns (i.e., what people need and want) and overall consumer demand.

Consumers place a premium on value and are extremely price-sensitive during tough economic times. In fact, discount retailers that offer more affordable alternatives such at TJX Companies (T.J. Maxx), Costco, BJ's Wholesale Club, Ross Stores, Kohl's, Dollar Stores, and Target have been some of the nation's best retail performers during this recession. In fact, these companies are experiencing some of their most profitable quarters in decades.

The Past, Present, and Future of Retail

The following is a conversation I recently had with a retail property owner. The owner said,

> My father acquired this building in 1964, and I've owned and managed it since 1978. This is the worst retail market I've experienced since we've owned the property. Our current rents have been reduced to 1986 levels, and we need to offer significant incentives to prospective tenants just to keep our occupancy at a decent level. Making matters worse, prospective tenants who want to lease vacant space from us can't obtain financing be cause of the constricted credit markets. It's just a horrible retail market right now!

As previously mentioned, investors who acquired retail real estate during the past six to seven years likely paid a premium—as they did with most other asset classes during that period. Investors bought on inflated pro formas that projected rising rents, declining vacancies, understated concessions and tenant improvement allowances (financial incentives given to new tenants to offset their up-front expenses). Retail investors not only overpaid during the past seven years, but they used significant leverage (75 to 95 percent loan-to-value) and short-term debt to make those acquisitions. Convincing banks to lend the vast majority of the capital required for commercial property purchases was not problematic in the old economy.

The Opportunity

During the boom, most retail investors pursued the same exit strategy. They'd buy an existing center or build one from the ground up. They'd make much-needed capital improvements on the existing center or complete construction of the new development. Afterward, they'd lease all the available space, stabilize the asset, and maximize the property's net operating income (NOI). Finally, they would sell the property for a handsome profit and immediately begin the search for the next project. Assuming they could execute the plan within the time allotted, their loans would not mature, and millions would be made after the sale. It was a relatively straightforward and lucrative strategy, if the market cooperated and the investor was reasonably competent.

Unfortunately, the market did not cooperate after 2007. Although the subprime debacle contributed to the collapse of residential real estate, the subsequent financial crisis was responsible for causing aftershocks in the commercial market—including retail real estate. When the current recession began to negatively impact retailers, shopping center owners began to feel the pinch. After all, when individuals lose their job, home, and hope for the future, they naturally stop spending. As consumer sentiment waned, so did retailers' income. A clothing store retailer shared the following with me: "I've been in business for 25 years and have always done well. During our very best years (2004 to 2007), we generated about $100,000 a month in revenue. Our revenue is down 70 percent in 2010! We've never seen anything like this. I'm not sure how much longer we can stay in business."

Eventually, thousands of retailers were forced to close their doors, and vacancy rates skyrocketed at shopping centers throughout the country. When the economy began its downward tailspin, businesses in general became leery of future expansion. It suddenly became increasingly more difficult to fill vacant retail space. National retail vacancy levels reached an 18-year high of 10.6 percent in the fourth quarter of 2009, according to real estate research firm Reis.

Retail Real Estate

Even highly profitable retailers that wanted to expand could no longer secure the financing required to open new stores. One of the problems was attributed to the faltering of the nation's largest source of credit: CIT Group Inc. provided financing to about 1 million small- and mid-sized businesses but filed for bankruptcy in late 2009. The credit market for most retailers evaporated almost overnight, and additional credit, therefore, no longer existed for store expansion. Moreover, no one has been able to fill the void left behind by CIT's departure from the marketplace.

Existing tenants have been requesting rent abatements from their landlords to survive the recession. Furthermore, prospective tenants have been demanding much lower base rents and significantly larger tenant improvement allowances (TIAs). Retail vacancy rates have been climbing while rents have been falling. All in all, the situation is bad for retail property owners, and it's only going to get worse before it improves.

One of my friends is the principal of a firm that owns more than 1.5 million square feet of retail space. He stated that his strategy for 2011 was essentially tenant retention. He wanted to maintain a 90 percent occupancy rate in his centers. The mandate he was passing down to his leasing agents was not to lose any more tenants! The primary emphasis wasn't on new leasing or increasing rents but, rather, on the retention of the existing tenant base.

Nevertheless, because many property owners can't sell their centers for more than the debt owed on them and refinancing isn't an option, the entire sector will continue to experience severe contraction. Until the employment rate improves and consumer and business spending increase, I don't anticipate a recovery in the retail sector. In fact, the recovery is unlikely to occur until 2013 or, perhaps, even later. That said, it's a great time to be buying if the numbers are right and you have patient money.

Consolidation

Expect the weak to be gobbled up by the strong. Investors with strong balance sheets and deep pockets will acquire companies that are unable to refinance their debt and are in poor financial condition (because of the dramatic deterioration of the market conditions).

Simon Property Group Inc., the largest mall owner in the country, made a $10 billion offer for General Growth Properties Inc. (GGP) in early 2010. This acquisition did not materialize but would have resulted in the coupling of the nation's two largest shopping mall owners. General Growth declared bankruptcy in April 2009 after several failed attempts to refinance its debt. Once again, too much leverage and too many overpriced acquisitions during the past few years are to blame for the company's downfall. Indianapolis-based Simon Property Group Inc., owns 382 properties in North America, Europe, and Asia and could make the acquisition using almost all cash. This is the epitome of Darwin's theory of "survival of the fittest."

The consolidation would have created a near-monopoly in the high-end shopping center sector. Most retailers were not in favor of this merger because they feared the overwhelming leverage a Simon/GGP union could have wielded in the marketplace. For instance, a retailer might be forced to lease at multiple centers just to gain access to a single location it truly desires. Also, rents might be artificially inflated in shopping centers if one company owned the majority of the nation's retail space at these traditional shopping centers.

Challenges of Owning Retail Real Estate

The U.S. retail sector is not for the faint of heart: Many small retailers find it impossible to compete with Walmart and Target.

Small retail stores are also facing increased competition from Internet retailers. The Internet reduces expenses for online retailers when compared to brick-and-mortar retailers. Many online retailers are not subject to increased operating expenses in the form of commercial property insurance, taxes, Common Area Maintenance (CAM) charges, annual rental bumps, employee salaries, and sales tax.

Moreover, it takes an average of 4 to 9 months to lease commercial retail space.

Novice commercial real estate investors don't realize the costs associated with securing a lease with a good-credit tenant. Assistance with the build-out cost (i.e., tenant improvement allowance) can run to tens of thousands of dollars alone.

Pop-Up Stores

I recently spoke with the director of leasing for a Simon Mall property, and he offered me two options: temporary leasing and permanent leasing. Property owners have discovered that they can fill unused space with removable kiosks and vacant space with temporary merchants. It has truly become a win-win situation for all parties involved.

One of the most recent trends for retailers is the pop-up or temporary store. Pop-ups have been instrumental in filling mall space during this economic slump. Pop-ups allow for short-term leases that could last 3 to 24 months. It offers retailers the luxury of being able to test concepts, locations, and product lines to determine whether success will follow. Retailers avoid signing a long-term lease that could prove financially disastrous if a particular model doesn't work.

Sometimes, it just doesn't make good business sense to sell year-round. After realizing that almost all of its business took place during the holidays, Hickory Farms moved almost exclusively to temporary stores and kiosks. Toys "R" Us and J.C. Penney use pop-up stores extensively throughout the United States.

Case Study 1

For 30 plus years, Redevco's mission has been to promote real estate development throughout southern Florida and to build strong neighborhoods and communities. The company specializes in retail, residential, and office projects as well as public-private ventures with local community development corporations. At the helm of this organization is Debra Kolsky, who has shepherded the successful construction, renovation, and management of more than 2 million square feet of shopping centers.

When prices were too high and cap rates too low, Redevco was not a buyer, and it kept to those principles during the entire boom. "Land prices were simply too high, and property owners were attempting to sell us on their unreasonable *pro formas*," Debra commented. Residential developers were competing for commercial sites for the first time. Her firm looked at a lot of deals during the boom but turned them all down because the numbers didn't make sense, and reasonable rents couldn't service the debt. The firm's strategy had always been to build for the long term and not for a quick sale. Redevco typically held onto the real estate assets it bought or developed.

In 2004, Debra realized the changes in the marketplace would require a different kind of thinking. Brokers became developers and added a level of competition that ultimately drove up prices. Redevco refused to chase deals and overpay.

When the market started to heat up, Redevco concentrated its business on private-public partnerships for infill projects. It pursued government and nonprofit projects. The city or the nonprofit would donate the land to the partnership, and Redevco would be responsible for the development. Both entities would retain a fair share of the equity in the project. The numbers made much more sense because there was no cost to the land component. During the boom, land prices escalated out of control, making commercial development a risky endeavor. Debra understood this, avoided the herd mentality, changed gears, and developed a strategy to avoid paying for land altogether.

Redevco mitigates the risk in several ways. It stopped giving personal guarantees in 2000. It preleases all its development projects before beginning construction. It invests its own cash in its deals and always avoids excessive leverage. A maximum of 50 to 60 percent LTV rates on all projects was permitted. "We will not be beholden to our banks," Debra noted. "We finance with 15-year notes and pay them off quickly. That's our recipe for success!"

Redevco prefers "mom-and-pop" retailers to big-box tenants. "The smaller, local tenants are our bread and butter," She added. Redevco prefers infill sites to undeveloped and unproven areas. Location, location, location is critical. The firm has been extremely successful in the inner city. Debra said, "The low-income urban core is great. Returns are just as good as any other place. We look for value-add deals on prime corners. We'll renovate the center and add security. Crime is everywhere and even higher in well-to-do neighborhoods. The nicest areas throughout the country are not immune to crime."

Debra admits that Redevco is now actively searching for distressed opportunities. They will return to the market at 10 caps. "There's likely another round of bad deals that will go bust, because there's so much money-chasing opportunities, and some of them will overpay. The sophisticated people are sitting back and waiting for real opportunities to present themselves," she explained.

Case Study 2

Sergio Delgado from Invest Real Estate Enterprises launched his career in real estate as a residential broker. During the boom, he would put well-situated land under contract and sell the deals at a significant

The Opportunity

profit. Suddenly, developers started to pull back and weren't buying his contracts in late 2007. "The easy money was gone," said Sergio.

Up to that point, he had worked diligently for five years selling land contracts, condos, townhomes, and single-family houses before transitioning into commercial real estate by acquiring his first retail property. Since that time, he has partnered with Ramon Mendez, and they have quietly added more shopping centers to their portfolio.

Sergio's mentor told him never to pay more than $100 a square foot for any property, and always buy at great locations (as they say, "Main on Main"). He also consolidated his search for new properties to a relatively small area—Miami-Dade County. He avoided chasing deals in nearby Broward or other parts of Florida.

Their strategy consists primarily of the following tenets:

- Put 30 percent or more down at closing.
- Pull money out of a project only if it doesn't exceed a 50 percent LTV.
- Be religious about managing your own properties—don't use management companies.
- Keep rents at or below market to keep centers full, because full centers drive traffic for all tenants.
- Cater to mom-and-pop retailers. It's better to lease to several small companies. It's far worse to have a big-box space of 30,000 square feet leased to one tenant. In a poor economy, if they leave your center, it will kill you! "Give me mom-and-pops every time!" In a good or bad economy, mom-and-pops pay the bills.

During the downturn, Sergio and Ramon's goal has been to maintain what they own and to live off the cash flow from their shopping centers. "We are hunkering down. We don't want to lose any tenants, and expect and hope the existing tenants pay at the beginning of the month," Sergio explained. To maintain occupancy, they have agreed to rent abatements and will work with tenants to keep them in place. "This is not the time to play hard ball!" he noted. Currently, they are nearly at 100 percent occupancy across seven properties with 140,000 square feet of retail space. Amazingly, they only have 800 square feet available for lease.

Case Study 3

This is a story about a Frenchman, Luc Bansay, who convinced the owner of a 120-year-old Parisian bakery chain with more than 300 locations worldwide to sell him the exclusive rights to expand the brand to the United States.

Whether you're a retail property investor, a franchisee, a tenant-rep broker, or a leasing agent for a shopping center owner, you need to have an intimate understanding of retailers. Luc's story will provide a unique insight into the franchising world and show you how a century-old business model with a stellar track record of success can ultimately fail if it doesn't effectively adapt to new markets.

Luc Bansay's family owned numerous shopping centers in Paris. In fact, Luc's uncle launched the family into the real estate business and learned the trade from the best in the business. Melvin Simon, founder of Simon Malls, happened to be his mentor.

One of the family's best-performing tenants in France was a bakery chain called Paul. It consistently did well each and every year. Luc eventually developed a close relationship with the founders of Paul, and in 2003 he was able to buy the license for the entire U.S. territory. His initial goal was to open 100 stores within five years.

According to Luc, the French concept had four key differentiating qualities:

- Paul attracts people all day long because it serves breakfast, lunch, and dinner.

The Opportunity

- Paul attracts the Starbucks crowd, but the average ticket price is much higher because of their food sales.
- Paul had a long history of success in Europe, and Americans like success stories.
- Paul bakes fresh bread in front of customers each day and offers a healthy alternative to fast-food models found in the States.

Luc's team selected Miami as its headquarters and opened the first store in 2004. The team spent $15 million to open just seven stores. "We should have opened 30 stores with that amount of money, but corporate wanted a certain image," Luc explained. The corporate image for Paul required Luc to spend extravagantly on the build-out of each location. It was more important that each location upheld the company's high-profile image. Profitability was secondary, according to Luc.

They were also forced into leasing larger stores than they really needed. Luc eventually realized that smaller was, in fact, better. He preferred grab-and-go food versus the full-service concept. Smaller stores also required less support. Bigger stores required a larger staff and more inventory, and they came with significantly more problems!

One of the standard prototypes was 2,000 square feet. It cost $2 million to build and generated $1.8 million in annual sales. It required a staff of 15 people.

However, a kiosk location, for example, was a fraction of the size and cost only $200,000 to build but generated $1 million in annual sales. It required only three employees and absolutely no inventory. This smaller model provided a far superior return on investment, but corporate was not in favor of smaller, less upscale stores.

According to Luc, Paul's corporate decision makers were obsessed with branding and image and not with profitability. "After all, when you're not spending the dollars, it's not really your problem, right?"

After several years of frustration battling with corporate mandates from Paris, Luc decided to sell (at a loss) his franchise rights and existing stores.

If you're considering buying into a franchise or leasing to one in your center, make sure you fully understand who is in charge. Luc took a great concept, invested millions, and devoted 6 years of his life to an endeavor that could not possibly work given the limitations and inflexibility mandated from the franchisor.

Gone Are the Days

Gone are the days when developers would just build a shopping center and wait for tenants to fill the space. No one is speculating on new retail space anymore. The only existing construction and development projects being built today are for specific users. A couple of years ago, retail developers needed approximately 10 percent down or zero percent down in some circumstances. Now, they need 30 percent or more, and their being required to come up with that amount of equity has become a major roadblock for most developers.

In a severely down market, value-add deals don't work as they once did. You shouldn't buy a center, make massive capital improvements, and then raise the rents on your struggling tenants. During a recession, tenants can't pay higher rents. Instead, stabilize your property and concentrate on the operating expenses as well as the retention of your existing tenants. Do what you need to do to cut costs until the economy improves.

Opportunity

Banks most certainly will consider making more commercial loan modifications because they don't have too many options other than becoming commercial property owners themselves. Inasmuch as banks are in the business of lending, most prefer to avoid direct ownership of real estate assets. Even if the monthly payments made to the lender are reduced, most banks will realize it's better to receive some form of payment—with the hope of eventually receiving a full repayment of the balance owed—rather than receiving no additional payments, foreclosing on the borrower, and being forced to liquidate at a significant loss (not to mention the legal fees involved). Many commercial borrowers might be able to eventually get back on track and pay off their loan. It therefore might benefit banks in the long run if they would be more amenable to loan modifications, especially if the economy is still lagging and the alternative options are not as favorable. Collaborating with borrowers to find a solution may be the bank's most prudent option.

If commercial lenders opt to extend loans that have matured and are in default, don't expect a bevy of distressed-buying opportunities in the retail sector. If, on the other hand, lenders decide to cut their losses, mark to market nonperforming loans, and clean up their balance sheets by liquidating, it would likely represent a tremendous opportunity for well-capitalized investors to identify distressed properties and acquire them at a significant discount to their fair market value. Buyers who can purchase and hold assets will most certainly profit when the market rebounds.

If you acquire a retail property that is not stabilized (i.e., less than 80 percent leased), you must be financially capable of weathering the storm until capital markets thaw out, consumer spending improves, and retailers begin to expand again. If you don't buy low enough and/or you use too much debt (assuming you can even source financing) for your retail acquisitions, you might regret making the acquisition too soon.

Either way, if you can acquire well-designed, well-located retail centers at steep discounts using a reasonable amount of debt, you will undoubtedly do extremely well in the next market cycle. Long-term prospects for this asset class are quite favorable, but the horizon for brighter days is still 3 to 4 years away. You must buy low enough so that the numbers make sense for you today and during the next few years because vacancy rates and rents will continue to slide. Be conservative with your analysis of prospective acquisition targets, and assume that the market will not rebound for a few more years.

12

Office Real Estate

In December 2006, an acquaintance of mine purchased a 10,000-square-foot office building on 70,000 square feet of land for $13.3 million. The property included 105 parking spaces. Three weeks after the closing, he received an unsolicited offer for the property of $15 million. Unfortunately, he couldn't convince his business partner to accept the offer—and a quick and headache-free $1.7 million profit! His partner was confident that a much bigger payday would be earned if they waited.

Within a few months, the owners negotiated a letter of intent to sell the property to Marriott. Marriott's plan was to convert the existing building into an extended-stay hotel for business travelers. The profit on the Marriott deal was a healthy $4 million, a much larger payday, as predicted by his business partner. Unfortunately, the market conditions began to deteriorate in 2007, and Marriott decided not to proceed with the transaction. The owners then were forced to consider alternative plans for the site. They concluded that a mixed-use property (residential and retail) would provide the best use for the site. A residential condo project of 200 units was proposed with several thousand square feet of ground floor retail. But that plan never materialized because of their inability to secure construction financing in a tight credit market. In the meantime, the vacant building sat idle collecting dust but still incurring ongoing expenses that included maintenance, taxes, and insurance. To make matters worse, the building was vandalized, and the air-conditioning systems were stolen. The vandals severely damaged the roof while extracting the air handlers, and the rain subsequently poured into the building causing even more damage to the interior of the property.

The mortgage was extended in December 2007, December 2008, and then again in 2009. Each time their lender agreed to an extension, they required the borrowers to pay down the loan with a substantial equity payment and provide additional collateral. The most current appraisal, however, had the property valued at only $3 million.

As I am writing this chapter, the owners had failed to make mortgage payments for 90 days and are officially in default. Because the borrowers don't have any additional capital to apply to the mortgage and they can't refinance the property because it's only worth $3 million (they still owed $7.1 million), the lender refused to extend the loan again. The borrowers are convinced that their only option now is to find a buyer and convince their lender to accept a short sale at a steep discount. A short sale or note purchase, however, presents its own set of unique problems. They will probably still be responsible for the deficiency (the difference between what is owed and what is paid to the bank) and could be pursued by the lender or buyer of the note. Also, in the event the lender forgives the amount not paid back, the IRS will classify the deficiency as taxable income. Last but not least, the borrower's credit will be damaged by a short sale to the tune of 200 to 300 points.

Bringing the Deal to the Lender

Banks and special servicers are inundated with problem loans. Note sales remain the lenders' best way to dispose of nonperforming loans. If a lender has lost its patience by continually extending a loan, it should be more receptive to a short sale. In fact, the lender's eagerness to sell a note at a discount might be more acceptable by a bank's board if the bank already extended the loan numerous times and has lost hope that a less costly exit strategy is forthcoming.

Most "bottom fishers" tend to think that the opportunity to find a distressed property will avail itself to them directly through the lender. However, what many inexperienced investors neglect to consider is that, when the bank makes the determination to sell a nonperforming note at a discount, the manager of special assets will contact its top five to ten customers and, unfortunately, you're not likely on that list.

Alternatively, you should be speaking directly with the distressed property owner so you can bring the property, your offer, and the owner directly to the lender in one easy-to-analyze offering. Working in unison with all the parties that have a vested interest in the asset will improve your chances of doing a deal. Moreover, you'll bypass the lender's top ten buyers because special assets will feel obligated to work with you. After all, you're bringing them the deal even before their loan officer sees it. I'm speaking from experience. This really works.

Case Study

I spent a year working on a project with Keystone Property Group, a Philadelphia-based real estate investment company with expertise in the office market. The firm had acquired a 300,000-square-foot office complex in 2007 and was in the midst of executing its value-add plan to the property. Keystone buys office buildings that are well-located but poorly leased and require significant capital improvements to attract higher-paying tenants. In other words, Keystone buys Class B or C properties in A areas. It buys the properties at a discount; makes the requisite upgrades, and leases at higher rents once the renovation has been completed. When existing tenants' leases expire, Keystone offers to extend their leases at much higher rates. The operational expenses for the property are reduced as much as possible while the rents are increased. Once the property has been stabilized and its net operating income maximized, it's time to sell. This strategy yields enormous profits and has been successfully repeated over and over again by Keystone.

After the tech-wreck and terrorist attacks in 2001, the office market was severely crippled. By 2003, the economy began to improve, and the demand for office space followed. Rich Gottlieb, a senior vice president at Keystone and a seasoned veteran with the company, survived several of these market cycles in the past. As Rich explained, "The office business is all about employees. The demand for office space is dependent on the economy. If the economy sours, so does the office market. It's a cyclical business with many ups and downs."

During the boom, however, the value-add cycle (the time it took from acquisition of a value-add deal to its disposition) was reduced from 5 years to 24 months. Because of this compression in the deal cycle, Keystone earned phenomenal returns from 2003 through 2007. By early 2008, however, the conditions started to change for the worse, and 2009 was an extremely challenging period. Gottlieb noted, "The market has been going down, and pro formas are now thrown out the window. The objective is to keep properties filled at the current market rents."

Apparently, 2009 was a decent leasing year for Keystone, but the leases signed were at much lower rates. When asked about the future, Gottlieb remained optimistic that the conditions for his business would improve within the next 12 to 24 months. "Companies need to make decisions for future growth. Companies have cut back very deeply, so I don't anticipate it getting much worse. Hopefully, we will turn the corner by 2011."

He did admit that numerous challenges confronted his firm in the new economy. "The rules have changed," he proclaimed. The capital markets and debt side of the business are not what they used to be. Very few lenders have an appetite for speculative developments (i.e., poorly leased properties in need of capital improvements). Banks just aren't lending for acquisitions on unstabilized properties. Without the ability to finance these types of properties, Keystone and other investors in the office sector can't achieve the returns they want; therefore, their value-add business model no longer works.

Keystone has had to reinvent itself in the new economy. It now is searching for less risky deals that don't require as much capital but would benefit immensely from Keystone's leasing expertise. Keystone hopes to buy office assets at reduced prices from motivated sellers; aggressively pursue their leasing plan; and ride future cap rate compression. Although Keystone wants to buy distressed assets from banks, they're not seeing any deals at the moment. Lenders are pushing loans out further and aren't foreclosing on office buildings. Gottlieb admitted that, "Banks are, in fact, better off extending for now. They still remember how much money investors made during the RTC days, so they want to get their money back this time around. We are not anticipating many distressed deal opportunities but continue to aggressively look."

Keystone's existing inventory remains problematic as well. The strategy during these tough economic times is to keep the properties leased and well maintained. Profits are eroding, but it's better to accept lower lease rates while minimizing vacancies than to suffer through this period with fewer tenants resulting from an attempt to maintain high lease rates. They have asked all their banks to extend their loans. So far, all of them have agreed. "They're not going to take down good sponsors," Gottlieb noted. That said, the new loan terms come with higher rates and require more collateral and additional equity payments to ensure their downside risk.

When asked to summarize what he had experienced during the past year and what he anticipates in the future, Gottlieb said:

- *Past:* Easier to pro forma in rising markets, not falling markets.
- *Past:* There were no acquisitions in 2009.
- *Past:* 2010 maybe no new acquistions again.
- *Future:* 2011 hopefully back in the game buying again.
- *Future:* Waiting for leasing and credit markets to rebound.

13

Residential Real Estate

History will forever link the current housing crisis to an abundance of easy-to-obtain debt and subprime loans. Because subprime borrowers used exotic loans (i.e., adjustable rate loans with 1 to 2 year teaser rates, negative amortization loans, and so on) to finance mostly condominiums and single-family houses, the value of residential real estate has fallen precipitously since the crisis began in 2007—a year that coincides with the first wave of those loans resetting to higher rates. Although the residential market was the first to falter, it will likely be the first to rebound when the economy recovers.

The run-up in residential prices was caused largely by the government's manipulation of the markets and its deregulation of the financial industry. After the dot-com bust and the terrorist attacks on the World Trade Center in 2001, the Federal Reserve lowered interest rates to avoid a deeper recession. Lower interest rates and more lax lending guidelines (due in large part to the government's desire to encourage home ownership) fueled the residential real estate bubble and created a house of cards that eventually crumbled and led to the greatest financial collapse since the Great Depression.

The term "flipper" became a commonly used term during the boom years. In fact, *Flip This House* became a popular TV series on A&E. This series depicted mostly inexperienced real estate speculators buying homes, quickly renovating them, and flipping them for a quick profit.

Flippers were making significant gains after just a few months of ownership. Some speculators bought contracts to purchase condos (typically requiring only 5 to 10 percent down) only to sell the rights to close on the unit(s) when the building was completed at some point in the future. Thousands of people (mostly in Miami, Las Vegas, and San Diego) stood in line during the first day of sales for the opportunity to buy a contract. Hundreds of units would sell out in a single day.

A *BusinessWeek* article published in 2005 highlighted the sheer madness of a market gone haywire:

> The latest sign of the Apocalypse: In south Florida, where housing speculation is white hot, some entrepreneurs have unveiled a pair of Internet-based exchanges—USCONDEX.com and CondoFlip.com—where individuals can buy or sell condominiums sight unseen. (Dean Foust, "Flipping in Florida," *BusinessWeek*, July 27, 2005; available at http://businessweek. com/the_thread/hotproperty/archives/2005/07/flipping_in_ florida.html).

Typically, value-add investors buy a property and make improvements to the asset. The value added to the residential property should exceed the cost to make the improvements. If all goes according to plan, the investor sells the property for a profit. During the boom, little was required in terms of adding value except for putting it right back on the market for resale. Prices increased at such alarming rates that many value-add investors found that their incremental improvements resulted in exponential growth in perceived market value. It was real estate on steroids. The values grew larger and larger and required less time and effort.

Homebuilders built more homes to keep up with the pace of demand. The largest homebuilders in the country, including D.R. Horton, Lennar Homes, and Pulte Homes, would all peak by 2005. A share of D.R. Horton's stock increased from $3.00 in 1997 to a high of $42.00 in 2005. Pulte Homes, the nation's largest homebuilder, saw its revenue grow from $2.33 billion in 1996 to $14 billion in 2005.

As prices skyrocketed, homes became less affordable, but financing them with low interest rates (or no-interest teaser rates) along with low down payments made it easier to buy. Because most real estate speculators believed that property appreciation would continue unabated, they were willing to pay higher prices just as long as the financing spigot remained in place.

One loan originator I know said, "I never made a loan that Wall Street didn't like." Although the loans were mostly toxic, banks were able to sell them off to the secondary market. In fact, most lenders that sold their mortgage loans assumed very little risk. They merely financed the loans (regardless of whether they believed the borrower could afford it) because they'd profit handsomely from each transaction. If the banks could process more loans, they could make more money. Period. The cycle continued for several years, but the preordained train wreck would eventually force the system to collapse.

By April 2007, subprime mortgages accounted for one-half of all mortgage-backed securities that were being issued. By that summer, the demand for mortgage-backed securities dried up, and the residential real estate market subsequently cratered. By September 2007, the bubble had, indeed, popped, but speculators who failed to liquidate their real estate holdings found themselves between the proverbial rock and a hard place. Prices were quickly declining, and qualified buyers were harder to find.

One of the leading brokers at one of the largest real estate practices in Fort Lauderdale informed me that 85 percent of all residential sales in Broward County were short sales or REOs (real estate owned) in 2009. If you were an average homeowner trying to sell your property under normal conditions, you had to compete with an avalanche of distressed properties that likely made your home look rather expensive by comparison. I knew people who were current with their mortgage but still desperate to sell. They eventually sold for less than their mortgage balance, and actually had to bring funds to the closing table to pay off the deficiency between the sale price and the outstanding mortgage balance.

Recovery

With residential values plummeting by as much as 55 percent in some areas, the rent-versus-buy ratios suggest that a recovery is forthcoming. In other words, home ownership is becoming more affordable as the reset in property values takes place. My crystal ball hints at modest growth in the residential market by 2011. Once it becomes as affordable to buy as it does to rent, demand will favor home purchases, and prices will stabilize once again. In a healthy market, average home prices do not exceed three to four times the median household income.

Caveat: The housing recovery, however, is subject to the health of the overall economy and in particular the rate of unemployment. The rate of recovery is also dependent on the area. Markets that didn't reach a fever pitch such as in Boston, San Francisco, Washington, D.C.,

Seattle, and New York will fare better than bubble-prone markets such as Miami, San Diego, Las Vegas, and Phoenix.

Buyers are swooping in to acquire distressed residential real estate in the hardest-hit markets. Homes that sold for $1 million in 2005 are now trading in short sales for $500,000 or less. Most investors are doing the math and buying when they can achieve a decent return on their investment (from a rental perspective). In other words, an acquisition can be justified if an investor acquires a property at a steep discount, and the existing market rents cover the mortgage, maintenance, taxes, insurance, and so on.

Nonspeculative investors are buying residential property on the basis of its return as a rental property. They realize that instant appreciation is no longer guaranteed but is an ancillary benefit of ownership. Speculators might settle for a breakeven scenario with the hope that the market eventually rebounds, and they sell for a profit at some point in the future. Both investors and speculators, however, should plan to hold their properties for at least the next 4 to 7 years before they can realize any significant gains.

As confident as I am that the sun will rise in the east and birds will fly south for the winter, I, too, am sanguine about the prospect that residential home values will recover. It's unlikely that we'll see 2005-like values any time in the immediate future; however, we'll eventually return to equilibrium—historical increases with annual appreciation in the 3 to 4 percent range.

Case Study 1

Ed Henkin is a neighbor of mine. He's also an honest, hard-working home builder and president of Edge Hill Homes. His projects can be found in the most prestigious neighborhoods of Miami, Palm Beach, and the Hamptons. As you can imagine, his homes are some of the finest in the country.

Ed is a fourth-generation real estate investor. His great grandmother used a $5,000 settlement to buy her first duplex in New York. She died in 1970 with an estate valued in excess of $1 million.

Ed's grandfather and father started making second mortgages to New York multifamily investors in the 1970s. During a recession, they began to construct their own portfolio of real estate holdings by fore-closing on some of their nonperforming loans.

Ed grew up in the family business managing several low-income apartment complexes in the Bronx. His father enjoyed the low end of the business. He once paraphrased Lincoln by stating, "God loved poor people. After all, he made a lot of them."

Ed eventually went to law school but had his heart set on build-ing. In 1988, at the age of 27, he found his first project—an old country farmhouse in the suburbs of Connecticut—that he renovated for his family.

Ed continued to work for his father, managing apartment build-ings, but he couldn't make enough money in that position to pursue his lifelong dream of building high-end homes.

Eventually, he moved to Westchester and fortuitously met a gentle-man in his 80s who happened to own a significant amount of land in the county. In fact, he was selling lots in a 10-home community but had managed to sell only two when Ed approached him.

He took a liking to Ed and suggested a partnership. Ed agreed to build a spec house on one of the lots and convinced the owner of the land to accept payment after the house was sold. As luck would have it, a friend hired Ed to build a custom home for her and agreed to build on his lot.

As he began to build, he started marketing the other eight lots using his custom home as a model. He convinced an all-cash buyer to purchase his second custom home. At that point, he was off to the races. He eventually built five houses in this development and, with a successful track record and the capital he had just earned, he bought vacant land and secured construction financing.

He built a home in Westchester, completed construction, and sold it shortly thereafter. At the time, it was the most expensive spec home sold in the area at $2.4 million.

Afterward, Ed and his family decided to venture into the Florida market. In 1988, he and his family relocated to Miami. Fortunately, he was able to buy his Florida house in cash. His first home was in a tony neighborhood in Coral Gables. The house was 5,000 square feet and had good "bones" but needed a major facelift. Ed managed to complete the entire renovation within six weeks, and his family moved in immediately. He then purchased two more lots in the same neighborhood.

He built spec homes on those two lots and waited for a sale. The real estate market was slowing down, so he decided to place everything he owned for sale—including his primary residence. He waited three months, but no offers came in. Then, suddenly, he received offers on all three properties.

He sold everything for a significant profit and acquired another home from a builder who was having a challenging time selling. Ed made some changes to the property, lived there for two years, and, once again, sold at a nice profit in 2004.

At the peak of the market, he sold his next project when it was only 50 percent completed. By 2005, however, Ed realized that something was drastically wrong. Vacant lots were selling for $1.8 million. It cost another $1.8 million to build a structure. He was into the project for a little over $3.6 million (including soft costs). The numbers were becoming unattainable for most buyers. In fact, to illustrate just how ridiculous the market had become, Ed bought a vacant lot for

The Opportunity

$1.8 million and sold it a few months later with architectural plans (the plans cost $75,000) for $2.6 million!

By 2005, there was a lot more risk involved because the numbers kept getting bigger. Million-dollar projects suddenly became $3 or $4 million investments.

Ed bought land in Palm Beach in early 2007. He built a 5,500-square-foot spec house on a double lot with ocean views. It was completed in early 2010. It's currently on the market for $5.8 million.

In parallel with the Palm Beach house, Ed partnered with an investor in the Hamptons to build a $16 million estate. Unfortunately, the construction loans matured before he could sell it, and the lender was pressuring him to pay off the balances.

When things started getting bad, he requested a meeting with his loan officer to inform his lender that he was running out of cash. He had done all his business with one bank and had always paid his loans in full. In fact, he was the bank's number one builder during the boom. Unfortunately, the equity in his projects was quickly dissipating, and his lender was getting nervous. Refinancing was not an option.

Ed suggested to his lender that he pay them in full when he sells the houses. The lenders suggested that Ed make interest-only payments now ($35,000 a month on the Hamptons home alone) and demanded cross-collateralization on each of the loans.

Unfortunately, Ed did not know how much time would be required to sell the two projects, given the current economic climate. Although Ed had personal guarantees on his loans, the bankers wanted greater security that the loans would be repaid. They requested cross-collateralization with his primary residence, an increase in the interest rates, and a pledge of interest with other assets that still had equity. This lender was playing hardball.

When you owe the bank a dollar, the bank owns you. But when you owe the bank a couple of million dollars, you (sometimes) own the bank. Ed decided to also play hardball, and the bank eventually acquiesced.

Ultimately, the lender agreed to extend his loans at the existing rates with the existing terms. Ed was the recipient of a life preserver that would allow him to stay afloat for another 12 months.

When asked about the future, Ed said, "The future is a bit uncertain. I just want to survive this storm. I know the market will eventually improve and I'll do well."

If Ed is able to sell his properties for the amount he considers they're currently worth, he'll make a decent profit and survive this downturn. If the properties can't be sold before the lenders call in the loans, he'll lose his entire initial investment and be on the "hook" for the deficiency should they sell the properties at a discount in a fire sale.

Ed reiterated his belief in the market and thought that the residential market would rebound by 2012. He's prepared to get right back into the fray by buying a lot at a steep discount and building with a two-year horizon to sell. He can duplicate his initial success by finding a motivated landowner who is willing to partner with him. After all, lot prices are coming way down, and the numbers are beginning to look more attractive again. If the market does correct itself and he's able to sell his properties for a profit and pay off the loans, he could be back in business by 2012 with his first profitable venture in more than 6 years.

Ed expressed a desire to live a simpler life. He needs much less than he has now and wants to live a more modest lifestyle with less overhead. I suspect that anyone who experienced financial hardship during this period will share a similar sentiment. In fact, this is a valuable lesson for all of us.

Case Study 2

Riley Smith of EWM is a residential real estate agent based in Miami, Florida. Riley is unlike 99 percent of most other Realtors because he's a creative thinker determined to change most of the paradigms established by his industry.

A local investor recently described him as a person "who will put the competition and especially the older and more established but less tech-savvy brokers out of business in this new economy."

Riley started selling residential real estate in 2000. He described the boom years that followed as a constant state of euphoria. It was not easy to obtain listings because properties sold so quickly, and the competition was stiff with discount brokers, so he concentrated his efforts on finding buyers.

"From 2003 to 2006, I was advising my buyers to offer at least the asking price for the homes that interested them. Properties would sell before they were even listed. In fact, we would often write contracts on the hood of a car as houses practically sold by themselves back then—sight unseen."

During those euphoric times, the demand outstripped the supply by a significant margin. Riley spent the majority of his time showing his clients around town to find the best house—not necessarily at the best price.

By late 2007, he began to sense that he needed to adjust his business model. At that time, he noticed that the real estate market was slowing down. His farm area averaged 45 homes for sale in 2005, but that number increased to 75 and then 100 in 2007. Buyers were pulling back in 2008 and were more reluctant to pay asking prices. He spent time with his team discussing the trends taking place in his industry and decided to act quickly to address the oncoming challenges.

"If you want to survive long-term as a Realtor, you need listings," Riley said.

To get more listings, he embraced technology to help advance his business and differentiate it from the competition. He started writing a real estate blog to garner attention from a larger audience. According to him, it was the best thing that ever happened, because 75 percent of his listings have originated from his blog during the past two years. The vast majority of his buyers resided outside his farm area because the locals weren't buying during the crisis.

When he launched his blog, it was ranked as the 650th listing on Google. Today, when you Google "Grove Real Estate," his blog is one of the first-page entries. According to Riley, his blog was the 35th-most-visited real estate site in the country. But he and his wife are required to spend 2 to 3 hours each day writing the blog. "Not everyone can do it. The old-school Realtors don't understand the importance of technology. It requires a lot of work, dedication, and money."

Riley understands that giving the information for free is absolutely essential. The old-timers hold the information close to their vest. They don't release it because they feel that information is their primary differentiator. But what they don't understand is that the Internet already gives most tech-savvy consumers the information they need. They just need someone to collect all of the information in one place and interpret the data for them. Whoever can do this for the consumer will do extraordinarily well for themselves.

As Riley likes to say, "The Internet has changed my business more than the crisis."

Also, he made a concerted effort to create a unique brand. On each of his For Sale signs, the words "Grove Specialist" appear. Perception became reality, and he is quickly becoming the dominant broker in this area.

Today, Riley spends 80 percent of his time securing new business (i.e., listings) and 20 percent of his time working the business (i.e., paperwork, touring with prospective buyers, managing his team, etc.). These days, buyers require significantly more time because they want to tour 35 homes as opposed to just two or three which is all that was necessary during the boom. It can be extremely time-consuming to conduct these tours, so he hired other sales agents to work with his buyers while he continues to oversee their work and develop the platform required to match buyers with sellers.

Admittedly, the competition is still fierce, but the less competent brokers have left the business, and only the good agents remain. Riley has, indeed, prospered during these tough times. He indicated that locals are back in the market buying properties again, and sellers want a dynamic Internet presence, so the blog remains his largest source of listings.

Here is a rundown of Riley's sales history:

2006: 30 homes sold

2007: 35 homes sold

2008: 37 homes sold

2009: 39 homes sold

2010: 55 homes sold

Riley predicts the following:

- Flat property value growth until 2012; values will start to grow by then.
- Limited new supply because there's no new construction.
- Condos and town home appreciation in his farm area will remain dormant for 3 to 5 years because of the excess inventory.
- Creditors' unwillingness to lend to condo buyers will remain an issue going forward.
- Lending guidelines at local banks will eventually become more lenient. "Small, local banks are more aggressive and more willing to lend."

Residential Real Estate

When the market rebounds and his area is flooded with new realtors again, he is not overly concerned because he has already secured the vast majority of the market share and is using technology like no one else is.

14

Multifamily Housing Units

The housing and financial crises were disastrous for multifamily operators because foreclosures and failed condo conversion projects added an abundant supply of new units to the existing inventory. The shadow effect caused by this tsunami of reverted condo units (condos that were reverted back to rentals) had an overwhelming negative impact on the rental market.

Renters had many more options to choose from so rental demand subsequently plummeted, and the increased supply of units depressed rental rates. I recall my property manager calling me one day in early 2008 informing me of the difficulty he had renting one of my buildings:

"Matt, we don't have granite countertops or stainless steel appliances. Renters expect these upgrades in their units because they're readily available for the same price elsewhere. If we want to be competitive, you might need to upgrade your units or reduce your rental rates."

The failed conversion projects down the street had been upgraded substantially with the intent to sell them as condos. When the market crashed, most developers (or their lenders) were left with empty condos that had to be transformed back to rental units, albeit luxurious rentals. The property owners who owned more traditional units (i.e., those with Formica countertops) were forced to offer prospective tenants free rent and lower rates in order to entice them to lease the less-desirable units. Otherwise, they couldn't compete with the rush of upgraded units coming onto the market.

In my estimate, 2008 and 2009 were the absolute trough years for the multifamily sector. One of my neighbors owns 8,000 apartment units in southern Florida. He is one of the largest owners of apartment units in the entire state. The occupancy rate in his portfolio in early 2007 averaged 96 percent, but by 2009 it had dropped to 87 percent. Meanwhile, his effective rents (rents less concessions) decreased dramatically. However, he, too, agrees that the fundamentals for the multifamily apartment market appear to be improving, and so he is preparing for a dramatic turnaround starting in 2011 and buying up properties at a discount.

Better Times Ahead

Multifamily will be one of the first real estate asset classes to recover. In fact, 2011 should be a spectacular year for apartment owners. Assuming that the U.S. economy slowly rebounds and the national unemployment rate improves, demand for rental units will soar to new highs. It has taken a few years, but the excess housing supply is being absorbed, and rents are stabilizing. According to the Case-Shiller Index, the bottom of the residential housing market occurred in late 2009 and values have been steadily increasing ever since.

The rental market has already improved and should show signs of steady growth by 2011. The year will usher in a new era with landlords having the upper hand, and it should remain that way for, perhaps, the next 5 years.

Multifamily Housing Units

The response we receive from our Craigslist rental ads is a fairly accurate (yet non-scientific) barometer for gauging the strength of rental demand in our farm areas. For example, in early 2009 we posted online ads for our rental units in Boston, and on average each one would generate only about 15 responses each week. A year later, we posted the same ads and received twice as many responses during the same time period and rented units twice as fast. Although the demand for rental units will vary from region to region and property to property, the trends (i.e., rental demand, rents, vacancy rates, time to fill vacancies, concessions, and so on) are quickly improving for multifamily property owners.

If retail follows rooftops, multifamily follows jobs. The soft rental market is for the most part a result of the nation's 10-plus percent jobless rate. Unemployed tenants have few options other than moving in with relatives or finding roommates to share their homes. That said, fundamentals will change for the better, especially when the labor market gains traction. Labor market experts suggest an increase in employment by late 2011.

Demand for apartments is increasing as people live longer, the echo boomers (the children of the baby boomers) complete high school or graduate from college, and immigrants continue to flock to our country. People need a place to live regardless of how poorly the economy is performing. Also, as individuals continue to suffer financial hardship resulting from foreclosures and bankruptcies, they will turn to apartment units as a more economical housing alternative. With homeowners awash in too much debt, the number of people looking for affordable housing will only increase. For all of these reasons, I am sanguine over the prospect for a dramatic improvement in the multifamily sector.

Supply: Lack of New Product

Very few apartment projects are being built on a national basis. The unavailability of credit for multifamily developers has prevented the construction of many new projects. Multifamily starts have been reduced to a trickle of what they used to be. Fewer than 100,000 units broke ground in 2009 and 2010. The apartment sector has experienced the lowest levels of new construction permitting since the 1950s.

Because of the credit crunch, the sector will benefit from an anemic supply of new projects during the next few years. Even as new construction begins in 2011, it will take a few years for those projects to be completed. Supply won't be able to catch up with demand until, perhaps, 2015.

Demand: Echo Boomers and Hispanics

About 35 percent of the U.S. population depends on rental housing. While the supply of new apartments is halted because of a lack of new construction, demand will increase from two main sources: the echo boomer generation and the U.S. Hispanic population.

The echo boomers are expected to be responsible for an increase of half a million new renters entering the market every year from now until 2020. Some experts estimate that the U.S. Hispanic population will grow from 35 million in 1999 to nearly 50 million by 2011. Moreover, the Hispanic population is quite young when compared to non-Hispanics. Most fall within the prime renter's age of 18 to 40. U.S. Hispanics are the fastest-growing segment of our population and will add significantly to the demand for rental units over the next several decades.

Two- to Four-Unit Buildings

While many bottom-feeding investors are searching for single-family houses or condos to acquire for investment purposes, I'd suggest that first-time investors consider duplexes, triplexes, and quads.

Two- to four-unit buildings tend to generate more rental income than a similarly priced condo or home. Moreover, properties with four units or fewer qualify for residential loans. Residential loans can be secured with less than 5 percent down (especially if the property is owner-occupied) and come with more flexible terms and conditions. By comparison, commercial loans—which require more than 20 percent down at closing—are used for properties with five units or more.

Time to Buy

It's an ideal time to buy a multifamily property. Interest rates remain low, and prices and cap rates are near pre-1999 levels. Many investors acquired apartment buildings at the peak of the market and are now losing them through the foreclosure process. The disagreement over property values between banks and buyers has created a stalemate in which fewer distressed transactions took place than originally anticipated. But the chasm in the bid-ask spread war has finally abated, and more deals are being completed.

Plan to hold any new acquisition for at 3 to 5 years. Flipping and condoing apartment buildings are no longer a viable exit strategy. Conditions now favor investors who want a long-term investment that generates a decent cash flow and gains value over time.

Traditional value-add strategies to boost a property's NOI must be modified. During challenging economic times, people aren't willing to pay an additional $300 a month for more bells and whistles. Tenants want an apartment in a good, safe location and are sensitive to price. The purchase price, therefore, is critical for investors. By minimizing the property's debt, you'll be able to better compete on price.

During this downturn, fortunes will be made by investing in distressed multifamily properties, so be sure to consider these opportunities very closely.

Refer to my book, *Investing in Apartment Buildings,* for a more in-depth review of this topic.

15

Farm Areas

I've written about farm areas in all of my books thus far. In fact, every time I'm a guest speaker at a real estate conference or I'm interviewed by the media about investing, I make a concerted effort to discuss farm areas. It's not a frequently discussed topic, but since novice investors encounter significant problems when they don't concentrate on a single farm area, when they chase cap rates out of state, and make "blind" investments, I make an effort to address this issue whenever possible.

A *farm area* is a well-defined geographical area where investors limit their property search. A farm area may be a single street, community, town, or city. When choosing a farm area, it's always best to select an area that is close to your home and/or place of business. It's also best to select an area that you're already intimately familiar with or an area that you intend to become intimately familiar with in the near future.

If you know every street, property, zoning regulation, future development project, and so on for a given area, you will have a competitive advantage over other investors who lack that local knowledge. Local knowledge will be critical to your success as an investor in real estate.

I receive countless e-mails from novice investors who want to chase cap rates in other states. Some broker sent them an e-mail with a great "deal" in some other part of the country. Perhaps they found a high-cap-rate listing on CoStar or LoopNet. They searched in their own community and could find only 5 percent cap rates, but in a city 1,000 miles away they were told that 10 percent cap rates exist. Unfortunately, they know absolutely nothing about this town (where higher cap-rate properties are in abundance) and so they plan a business trip to tour the area. After spending 3 days in this new city, they feel confident that they know the lay of the land. After all, they visited town hall, spoke with the locals, ate in nearby restaurants, and stayed at the most popular hotel. Now it's time to make a multimillion-dollar investment. Countless investors have done precisely that, and most have failed miserably.

Your success rate increases dramatically if you limit your property search to a specific location, assuming, of course, that you know your farm area extremely well.

As an example, let's say that you live in Los Angeles and that the properties you're analyzing don't exceed a 7 percent cap rate. Suddenly, you're made aware of a 10 percent cap-rate deal on a property in New Mexico. You think to yourself, "It's only a few hours' plane ride away, and the property will produce significantly more cash flow than the assets I'm considering in Los Angeles. I should buy it!"

Big mistake!

That 10-cap deal quickly becomes a 4-cap nightmare because you didn't know what you were getting yourself into. A local will know the difference between Main Street and High Street. After all, one or two blocks in the wrong direction can be devastating to your bottom line. Don't chase cap rates in other towns. Avoid the illusion of higher cap rates and superior returns in places far from home. Leave national investing to the professionals. They have the resources, local knowledge, and deep pockets to invest in all 50 states. Noninstitutional entrepreneurial investors should, in my opinion, always invest in their own backyards.

Case in Point

There's a beautiful and quaint part of Miami called Coconut Grove. One of my business associates from Boston recently expressed interest in owning retail property there. He pulled a demographic report for the Grove and was encouraged by the data. He walked the area and noticed there was ample pedestrian traffic on the streets. The restaurants seemed full. He realized that the Grove was close to the University of Miami, and students frequented the area at night. It seemed like an ideal place to invest. However, what he didn't know would have changed his mind:

- The area's anchor, CocoWalk, was in foreclosure, and the movie theater had closed for renovations.
- The local playhouse was closed, and there were no immediate plans to reopen it.
- The convention center was no longer a major draw and required a major renovation to upgrade the facility for future use.
- Competition from other developing neighborhoods (Mary Brickell Village, south Miami, Miracle Mile, and downtown) had recently siphoned traffic away from the Grove.

As a local investor, you would have been aware of all these factors and realized that the area was in decline. A savvy local investor would pursue acquisitions in this area only because of the possibility of capturing a great deal in the downturn. Personally, I am confident in the area's long-term viability, so an investment made today at a steep discount from a motivated seller should yield good returns in the future. But my point remains the same. You must know the local area extremely well (regardless of whether you're buying an apartment building or a shopping center) to fully understand the dangers and opportunities in each local market.

If you personally knew the shopkeepers, the local developers, and the property owners, you would have known that they were suffering financially. As an outsider, you see what you want to see and risk making a "blind investment" because you lack information. Don't get burned chasing cap rates in "foreign" places. Know your market like the back of your hand and stay close to home, especially if you're an inexperienced investor. Admittedly, it can be frustrating if you live in a large metropolitan area where demand for good investment properties remains at a premium, even during the downturn. However, mastering your farm area and finding those needles in the haystack are essential to your prosperity.

16

Community Anchors

My two farm areas are Boston and Miami. Although the housing crisis has affected Florida more than New England, both areas have experienced significant downward pressure on property values, rents, and occupancy rates.

That being said, real estate values remain very strong in areas that are in proximity to hospitals, universities, and other community "anchors." As 80 million baby boomers reach retirement age, the need for medical services will only heighten. Hospitals will continue to expand and prosper financially during the recession.

In fact, the Longwood Medical area of Boston is known as the health-care district for New England. Brigham and Women's Hospital along with Children's Hospital serve as anchors for this area. The hospitals continue to acquire land and buildings around them as they plot out their next 100,000-square-foot expansion because the doctors, nurses, facility managers, and personnel who work at these hospitals need places to work, live, and play. In fact, they will pay a premium to

The Opportunity

have an office or home close to the hospital. The increased demand for real estate in proximity to hospitals will most definitely enhance property values.

The same can be said about universities and colleges. Boston is fortunate to have 50 or more institutions of higher learning in the area. MIT, Harvard, Boston College, Boston University, Wellesley, Babson, University of Massachusetts, and so on aren't closing their doors in the next 100 years. As the 75 million children of the baby boomers (generation Y) apply to colleges throughout the country, university enrollment will expand dramatically. I know that the University of Massachusetts Boston witnessed a 25 percent increase in enrollment during the past four years.

With more students going to college these days, more professors and staff will be required to service the burgeoning student population. More people in general in or around colleges will equate to greater demand for the real estate surrounding campuses. Universities may need to expand their campuses to build more offices and classrooms, and they'll pay a premium for that real estate. Students and faculty will pay a premium to live within walking distance of campus, and the demand will continue for at least the next decade.

I have a good friend in Boston who spent the past decade investing in apartment buildings that were adjacent to universities. He rents by the room, provides free Internet connectivity, and furnishes the rooms for his tenants. His properties are always within walking distance of campus. He rarely has a vacancy and would never consider selling one of his properties. "They throw off too much cash flow and are relatively headache-free," he says.

The University of Miami (UM) and Florida International University (FIU) are the two major centers for higher learning in Miami. UM is a private university with approximately 15,000 students. FIU is a public university with an enrollment of about 40,000 students. Office, retail, and multifamily housing continue to do well if they are situated around either UM or FIU. A 404-unit apartment complex called Red Road Commons was recently constructed across the street from UM. Their rents are approximately 20 percent higher than the nearby competition but they remain 100 percent leased. There's not one vacant unit! The real estate market might be in great despair 10 miles away from these community anchors, but if it's within walking distance of either campus, values and rents have actually appreciated during this crisis.

For the past year, I've been trying to lease several thousand square feet of retail space from a shopping center directly across the street from FIU. It's a Publix-anchored center with more than 150,000 square feet of retail space. Guess what? It never has any vacancies. I contact the leasing agent every month, and the response never changes: "I'm sorry but we don't have any vacancies." If you drive 10 miles east, a similar center has a 15 to 20 percent vacancy level. The same phenomenon holds true for real estate demand in Cambridge. MIT and Harvard are such big draws that office, retail, and multifamily continue to thrive. No vacancies!

The president of Ohio State University (my alma mater), Gordon Gee, was quoted in a recent *Time* magazine article as saying, "In a world where brainpower outstrips muscle power, where innovation trumps conformity, where the nimble and creative stand to inherit the Earth, higher education is the key to the next American century. Colleges and universities are the catalyst of economic development. Classrooms and labs are today what mines and factories were a century ago: America's regional economic powerhouses, one of the few certain engines of growth in good and bad economic times."

Whether it's a local university, a hospital, a new baseball park, or a transportation hub, find yourself an anchor in your community and buy as close as possible to it. If the anchor does well, your real estate will also do well.

17

How to Add Value to Real Estate

Adding value to income-producing real estate requires a brief explanation of the real estate stack.

On evaluation of all potential acquisition targets, it's necessary to determine whether they are worth your investment capital. The real estate stack is the most basic of quantitative models that allows investors to determine the net operating income (NOI) for any given property. Once the NOI for an income-producing property is determined, the value can be derived, and that asset then can be compared to any other real estate investment opportunity.

Before you consider spending time touring a property, you should create an analysis of the asset based on the stack. Given your findings from this simple financial model, you can determine whether the property warrants a site tour.

Real Estate Stack (or Operating Statement)

Potential gross income (PGI)

(Less) Vacancy and collection (V&C)

(Plus) Other income (OI)

(Equals) Effective gross income (EGI)

(Less) Operating expenses (OE)

(Equals) Net operating income (NOI)

(Less) Debt service (DS)

(Equals) Before-tax cash flow (BTCF)

The Stack Explained

The potential gross income (PGI) of a property is the amount of annual rental income a property should (under ideal conditions) generate.

Assume that we have a 100-unit apartment building and that each unit rents for $1,000. The PGI equals $100,000.

Vacancy is shown as the average percentage (of the PGI) that the property is expected to remain vacant throughout the year. Collection losses amount to uncollected rent from existing tenants. Let's assume it's 5 percent or $5,000.

Other income (OI) amounts to revenue that is not based on unit rental income. OI could be generated from garage rentals, pet fees, rental of storage space, and so on. If 100 unit owners pay $100 a year toward storage space, OI = $10,000.

Effective gross income (EGI) is the amount of revenue you expect the property to produce each year. It is PGI less V&C plus OI:

$$\$100{,}000 - \$5{,}000 + \$10{,}000 = \$105{,}000$$

Operating expenses (OE) include all property-related expenses attributed to ownership. Some common operating expenses include advertising, insurance, taxes, repairs, reserves for replacements, maintenance, utilities, and so on. Operating expenses do *not* include debt service.

Assume $40,000 in operating expenses.

Net operating income is the Holy Grail for all investors because it represents the basis for comparison, assuming debt is not a factor. It represents the property's income before paying debt and income taxes:

$$NOI = EGI - OE, \text{ or } \$105,000 - \$40,000 = \$65,000$$

Annual debt service (DS) is the sum of all the mortgage payments for the year. The annual debt service includes both the principal and interest payments on an annualized basis.

Before-tax cash flow (BTCF) represents the gain or loss realized by the investor for the year. It does not consider taxes on that income.

The property analysis would look like this:

Annual Property Operating Statement

Potential gross income	$100,000.00
– Vacancy and collection	$ 5,000.00
+ Other income	$ 10,000.00
Effective gross income	$105,000.00
– Operating expenses	$ 40,000.00
Net operating expenses	$ 65,000.00
– Debt service*	$ 30,000.00
Before-tax cash flow	$ 35,000.00

Now that you understand how to create a property income statement, you're prepared to better comprehend how to add value to your investment property. If you plan to sell the property, the NOI must be maximized, to achieve the highest possible price at the time of the sale.

*Debt service assumed.

The Opportunity

To maximize NOI, you must improve all the factors that influence NOI including:—PGI, V&C, OI, and OE.

Increase the rents, and NOI goes up. Reduce vacancy and collections, and NOI increases. Increase storage fees or start charging for Internet access, and NOI can climb. Reduce operating expenses (OE) by negotiating a rate reduction with your insurance carrier, and NOI will be positively affected. Do all these things, and watch how the NOI improves and the property's value soars.

Let's assume that the average cap rate in your area for the asset class in question is 8 percent.

If your property's NOI is $65,000, the value of the property is $812,500 ($65,000/.08).

Now let's assume that you spent the past year working on your property so that NOI increases by $20,000 to $85,000.

The property is now worth $1,062,500. That's a $250,000 increase in value!

Concentrate like a laser on the stack and make improvements in every category that affects NOI, and your property will realize what's referred to as "forced" appreciation. Value-add deals are properties that can increase in value based on incremental improvements by ownership.

If holding the property for its cash flow over the long term is the goal, you should execute a plan to increase NOI (as discussed above) along with a strategy to reduce your annual debt service obligation. There are three principal ways to reduce annual debt payments:

- Refinance the property to a lower rate.
- Pay down the mortgage with larger equity payments and refinance.
- Pay off the mortgage and eliminate debt payments altogether.

If you're a real estate investor, then you're in the value-add game. Your job is to think of new ways to create additional value so as to consistently maximize NOI and cash flow.

Refer to my book *Investing in Apartment Buildings* for an in-depth review of specific strategies that add value to multifamily assets.

Case Study

Seth Gadinsky is the principal of Gadinsky Real Estate, LLC. He's a real estate investor and broker based in Miami. Seth buys vacant land (especially in areas shadowed by Walmarts) and develops the land for use by national retailers. The amount of rent that retailers are willing to pay largely determines what he can pay for the land. He won't buy land unless he has a lease in hand. Seth specializes in locating sites that retailers want and can afford. And he is very good at adding value to land by securing the requisite permits, rezoning the land (if necessary), and developing properties for national high-credit tenants. Let's say that a 2-acre lot is worth $1 million. How much is that 2-acre lot worth if Walgreens would construct a 15,000-square-foot store and pay $50 a square foot NNN (the tenant pays for the taxes, insurance, and common area maintenance) or pay an equal amount for a ground lease?

That property would generate $750,000 in NOI (assuming all expenses are paid by Walgreens). Using an 8 percent cap rate, it's worth over $9 million.

When times were good, Seth's model worked like a charm. The market, however, changed for the worse in 2008. Walgreens started canceling projects that were approved at the local level, and other national retailers also pulled back.

"Changing my model wasn't the best course of action because my strategy still works in good times and bad. In bad times, it just happens a lot slower," Seth says. Single-tenant, build-to-suit projects are fee-based, so there's always a profit to be earned if he can match the right real estate with the right tenant.

The Opportunity

Seth feels that future opportunities lie in the existing product because "New shopping centers aren't penciling out. 2011 should be better than 2010. I'm going to sift through all my deals and start over in 2011."

18

The Local Advantage

If you're a local high-net-worth investor competing with institutional groups for multimillion-dollar commercial properties, you might fear these deep-pocketed titans of the industry. Your fears, however, are not warranted. In fact, one of the most active sellers of mortgage notes in Florida sold less than 20 percent of its nonperforming commercial paper to institutional players as of late-2010. The predominant share of deal flow (approximately 80 percent) from this particular lender was sold to local investors who had the ability to move quickly, conduct their due diligence in a timely manner, and possess sufficient capital to buy in cash.

I spent 2 years courting private equity groups, thinking that they held the Holy Grail to the acquisition of institutional-grade properties. I eventually realized that all their corporate jets, extravagant business expense accounts, and Harvard-educated analysts didn't equate to meaningful deal flow. In fact, they were slow to analyze properties, slow to understand local market dynamics, slow to determine property values, slow to make decisions, and never offered equity to dealmakers.

Conversely, experienced owner-operators who earn their livings locally have the ability to make quick decisions without board consent or a 100-page appraisal report. Owners of locally based real estate investment firms (that already own numerous properties in the area) can make a determination regarding value and submit offers that don't need to be retraded upon further inspection of the property. Local investors are able to conduct their due diligence in a more expeditious way because they are intimately familiar with the market.

Some private equity groups I've dealt with in the past regularly flew planeloads of executives into town to inspect prospective acquisition targets. I know for a fact that one company spent more than $100,000 in 2 months to complete the due diligence on a single commercial asset that I was working on. A local owner-operator, however, spent less than 10 days on site and not more than $10,000 in due diligence to purchase that same property. In the end, the local investor closed on the property in just 2 weeks.

Local investors have the advantage of proximity—only a car drive versus a plane ride away from an acquisition target. They have the advantage of being able to establish and maintain an ongoing and constructive relationship with the local bank that's selling the property. Local investors, for example, have the advantage of knowing precisely what current market rents are (mostly because they own similar properties in the same area) and don't require a formal rental analysis of comparable properties to make those determinations. They also don't require unanimous board consent to make an offer. Whom would you rather work with?

The fear of competing with private equity firms and hedge funds should not discourage you from pursuing larger deals in your farm area. I personally witnessed a multitude of transactions that could not be closed by these companies. In fact, most distressed assets sell to the quiet-but-patient local owner-operator who can make a relatively quick decision about a property and can deliver the "goods" at the closing table. In fact, several lenders I deal with today have a short list of five or fewer buyers they call when a distressed real estate asset is ready to be sold. And as you might suspect, that short list consists of mostly local investors with a track record of success with the lender.

Part 4

The Future

19

Credit Markets

U.S. banks have lost billions during the past few years. They made questionable loans to individuals who didn't have the ability to pay them back. In fact, most subprime borrowers lacked the credit, income, and assets to qualify for their loans. Nevertheless, the banking community bent over backwards to provide unqualified borrowers sufficient debt to purchase homes they could ill afford. Lenders also encouraged homeowners to extract additional capital from their properties (as if the property was a piggybank) in the form of home equity loans. This additional capital fueled consumer consumption and debt to greater heights. Lenders also provided heavily leveraged loans to real estate speculators who acquired income-producing properties with very little of their own equity. During the boom, nearly every loan applicant qualified for a mortgage, business line of credit, or home equity loan. Credit was plentiful and easy to obtain, and overleveraging became an acceptable business practice.

The Future

Unfortunately, the lax lending practices were the cause of the housing crisis and subsequent financial meltdown. Too much mortgage debt caused the U.S. economy to fall into the worst economic recession since the Great Depression. As loans reset and homeowners lost their jobs because of the faltering economy, debt-laden Americans realized that they couldn't keep up with their poor spending habits. Ultimately, lenders were left with a sea of bad loans that could never be repaid. The crisis served as a wake-up call to the banking industry. If it wants to survive this fragile economic crisis, it had better change its ways.

Banks that have managed to survive the residential housing collapse are now bracing themselves for an aftershock—failing commercial property loans. Lenders are anticipating a second wave of defaults before conditions improve. Because of this concern, banks have tightened their lending standards and are adhering to significantly tougher qualifying standards. These new lending guidelines will probably remain in place for the foreseeable future.

It is unlikely that lenders will return to the irresponsible activity that was so common during the boom years (at least not for a long time). Instead of financing a property with a 90 to 100 percent LTV, lenders are requiring 20 to 30 percent down. They are demanding that buyers have sufficient equity in a property so that, if values continue to fall and the borrower stops making payments, the banks won't be forced to liquidate at a price less than the balance owed. In other words, lenders will mitigate their losses by requiring borrowers to come to the closing table with more of their own cash.

In many other instances, banks have stopped lending altogether. For example, one of the most common complaints I hear from shopping center owners is that their prospective tenants can't secure financing to build out their space. Small businesses are finding it difficult to obtain loans even for working capital. Retailers with profitable business models (even during the recession) and successful track records cannot find a bank to lend them the capital needed for expansion. Construction loans are impossible to find, and few lenders will consider making a loan unless the borrower has a significant down payment, sufficient collateral, an exceptional credit rating, and a lengthy track record of success. That's precisely why cash is king right now. If you don't require debt to make acquisitions, you're in an enviable position to buy at historically low prices. If you don't have the readily available cash but still want to acquire real estate, then you must find equity partners who want to invest in your projects. Make them limited partners and give them a preferred return on their capital. In other words, they get paid before you get paid. Family, friends, and business partners can provide the equity you need to get started. Equity partners provide the down payment, and are allocated a percentage of the annual cash flow and equity in the deal. Try to avoid raising additional debt from outside sources, though, because you don't want to be burdened with extra payments beyond the principal mortgage. If you succeed, your limited partners will receive a nice return on their capital and likely invest more in your next project.

Perhaps the phrase "no money down" will eventually disappear from the American lexicon. If you're a budding, young investor who wants to get into the real estate game, but you don't have a job or savings, please don't turn on the television after 1 a.m. I don't want a late-night real estate infomercial guru to convince you that buying properties and making millions is possible if you have absolutely no savings, source of income, or capital to invest. No-money-down investing is just bad advice. The exception, of course, is finding equity partners (as discussed above) that provide the capital while you provide the sweat.

Americans spent during the boom as if there was no tomorrow. There was an absolute disregard for living within a budget and investors failed to honor the tried-and-true fundamentals of real estate investing. Rather, they bought on speculation, expecting property values to increase regardless of the changing times. The rules of the new economy will challenge our society to live and invest within their means—and that will surely benefit everyone.

20

Creating a "Cash Cow" in Order to Buy Real Estate

If you've read all the chapters thus far, you should realize that zero-down deals no longer exist. Investors will need a 20 to 30 percent down payment to acquire most investment properties. For example, a $1 million purchase price will likely require a $250,000 down payment. So, I hear you ask: How on Earth will I find that much capital?

As previously discussed, you can source those funds from your friends and family. You can introduce the deal to other investors and inquire about the possibility of a joint venture if they provide the capital needed to get you into the deal. Or you can dip into your own savings to finance the acquisition (assuming you have the capital). If you don't have an extra $250,000 in your trust fund, you'll need to earn it before buying. This chapter introduces you to the notion of making money in another industry so that you can afford to buy real estate on your own.

Most high-net-worth individuals actively invest in real estate to diversify their portfolios. They might make their fortune in some other line of work but find that stocks and bonds don't completely meet their long-term financial goals and that greater diversification is required. Therefore, they tend to invest in income-producing real estate in order to achieve higher returns and a healthy passive income stream. They can acquire real estate because they have the capital to do it. You, on the other hand, may not possess the requisite funds needed to buy, but if your primary goal is to own income-producing real estate, you must find a way to raise capital.

Of course, I wouldn't dare attempt to suggest what business to start. There are far too many ways to generate money, so instead I'll share with you a true story from a person who launched a successful business and invested the profits in real estate. Perhaps, you then can glean some insight from this case study and duplicate his success.

Case Study

I met David Ivler in early 2010. He owned several retail properties in Miami, and we were working together to reposition one of his centers with national tenants. After a few weeks, I realized that he had an interesting background for a real estate investor. Although he was a highly educated, articulate, and amiable person, he took a slightly unusual path to real estate stardom.

While he was in his second year of law school at the University of Miami, he sold carpets to students who were living in the on-campus dorms. His carpet business was successful because he offered delivery and a custom installation. His company would cut the wall-to-wall carpet for each student's room and install it. Although it was a seasonal business, David had caught the entrepreneurial "bug," so he continued to pursue more money-making ventures.

Back in the 1980s, futons had just been introduced to our country from Japan, and they were extremely popular furniture pieces, especially on college campuses. One of his father's friends happened to be in the futon business in New York. This businessman was impressed by David's entrepreneurial spirit, so he asked David to be his business partner in Miami. With $20,000 of merchandise and a $5,000 capital investment from his father, David opened his first store near campus and called his company Futon Distributing, Inc.

He leased an 800-square-foot space and advertised his business in the local paper. He placed a sample futon in the display window of his retail shop—and it continually sold before he could get his store stocked with inventory. During his first 5 months of business, he sold $100,000 worth of merchandise In fact, he didn't have a storage room, so he had to schedule deliveries for new inventory every day to replenish what he had sold. Business was booming, so he began to search for another location. At the time (1988), South Beach (SOBE) was less developed than it is today, so rents were relatively inexpensive. But the people in SOBE were young and hip, and that made it an ideal place to sell this product. David found a large space on the corner of 5th Street and Washington Avenue, a main thoroughfare on Miami Beach, and he called it the "Warehouse Outlet Store" for futons.

The warehouse outlet store was even more profitable than his first location near the UM campus. The outlet realized a steady growth in income every month because it offered a trendy, unique product no one else was selling at that time. His futons had an attractive price point, and they served the dual purpose of being both a couch and bed.

After graduating from law school, David was able to dedicate all his time to the futon business. In 3 years, he opened 10 more stores in Miami. Within a few short years, his business was generating more than $1 million in revenue with average sales of $500 a customer. He eventually opened a 1,000-square-foot accessory store in 1992 that surprisingly generated $700,000 in revenue during its first year.

It wasn't all easy, though. He had to contend with damaged delivery trucks, break-ins at stores, internal theft, warehouse theft, and delivery theft. He survived Hurricane Andrew—a category 5 hurricane that destroyed two of his stores, along with the inventory, plus billions of dollars' worth of southern Florida property.

Nevertheless, business was booming, and further expansion was required to keep up with sales. He searched for more warehouse space to accommodate the pace of his business. He started looking for spaces in South Beach. One day, he noticed a rather unassuming-looking property with a For Sale sign on the building's facade. The owner wanted to sell the 7,000-square-foot property for $400,000. He was also willing to take just $50,000 down and hold paper for the remaining balance owed, using the building as collateral. This became David's first corporate headquarters and his first real estate purchase. He kept on buying buildings where he could locate new futon stores. He moved his storage facility off South Beach (where rents were increasing rapidly) and relocated it to a new building he purchased farther inland. Then, he leased the large facility on South Beach and made a nice profit.

During the course of the next several years, David continued to acquire more buildings for his futon business. In 1992, he acquired a small strip mall on South Beach for $500,000. He renovated the center, investing another $200,000. He leased the center for the next decade, and it was a highly profitable venture, grossing $350,000 during the peak years. In 2007, he sold the property for $5.1 million—a very nice payday after 15 years of ownership.

Eventually, the futon business started slowing down, but his real estate empire was speeding up. He bought some more retail properties along Biscayne Bay. They were all value-add deals. He'd buy them at a discount, renovate them, and lease them. Meanwhile, he winded down the futon business and became a full-time landlord and real estate investor.

Creating a "Cash Cow" in Order to Buy Real Estate

By happenstance and necessity, David got into real estate to grow his futon business. He soon realized that the landlord business was even more profitable than the futon business. Today, he owns 36,000 square feet of retail space with a maximum leverage of 50 percent. All of his properties generate a positive income stream. He is searching for more properties in the area and wants to buy opportunistically during the recession.

The key to life, according to David, is to have flexibility with your job and enjoy financial independence and the liberties it offers you and your family. Although real estate has provided superior returns when compared to his futon company, he is grateful to his futon business because it allowed him to get into the real estate game. He made a healthy living with futons but made his fortune with real estate.

David graduated from law school in 1989 and since that time he has accomplished all the goals he set for himself. He made all the money he has ever wanted. "My greatest accomplishment, however, is having a house on the water and living the ultimate Florida dream—a 15,000-square-foot oceanfront house with a lovely boat parked in front."

"Now comes the hard part—holding onto everything I've made!"

21

The No-Debt Alternative

Private equity groups, Real Estate Investment Trusts (REITs), and other institutional investors claim it's impossible to achieve their desired internal rate of return (IRR) without leverage. The typical return accepted by most institutional investors ranges from 17 to 25 percent. U.S.-based institutional firms rarely acquire real estate unless they can apply leverage to their financing.

Allow me to illustrate the power of leverage:

- Purchase price: $1,000,000
- Equity: $200,000 (20 percent)
- Debt: $800,000 (80 percent)
- Assume the property increases in value by 10 percent (or $100,000) in 1 year and is immediately sold. The sales price is $1,100,000.

- Profit: $100,000 (not considering closing costs, legal, brokerage fees, etc.)
- Return: 50 percent (100,000/200,000)

If the buyer made an all-cash purchase, the return would amount to only 10 percent. ($100,000/$1,000,000). Note: This is a very simplistic example used for illustrative purposes only.

I am not questioning the merits of leverage in real estate investing. However, I have begun to doubt its efficacy for noninstitutional investors who are consistently wiped out by the ebb and flow of market cycles. Because real estate is not liquid and it takes time to sell, the average real estate investor tends to lose a good portion of his equity when the market collapses (which is approximately every 8 to 12 years). Family fortunes are decimated, and dreams are dashed. There are an inordinate number of people who lost everything in this downturn, including their homes, boats, second homes, cars, college savings for their kids, and, perhaps, most important, their motivation to start over again. Even some smart, experienced investors lost what they had spent a lifetime building.

Most investors tend to think that more properties means more money and a greater net worth. However, this mindset doesn't always lead to the most optimal long-term strategy. Bigger doesn't always equate to a better financial position for most noninstitutional investors. A sounder strategy is to buy good real estate assets in great locations from motivated sellers. Then renovate the properties, lease them at market rates, and pay off the mortgages as soon as possible. Buy with the intent to hold for the next 30 years. When you finally pay off the mortgages, the properties will then generate an impressive cash flow each year.

Would you like to create a significant passive income stream from your real estate holdings to sustain your family through retirement and pay your kid's and maybe even your grandchildren's college tuition? Keep in mind that owning 50 buildings that are highly leveraged is usually not nearly as profitable as owning 10 buildings free and clear.

The No-Debt Alternative

A mortgage is like a deadly cancer. Get rid of it. Extract it as soon as possible. A prudent financial goal is to increase your cash flow by paying off your mortgages. I have a good friend who owns seven properties in Boston. He says that he could significantly increase the size of his portfolio if he wanted to, but he owns the buildings mortgage-free. The cash flow from his small real estate empire is more than ample to provide a nice lifestyle for his entire family. He no longer needs to work and has found greater balance in his life.

Another acquaintance of mine owns 10 very successful restaurants in New England. He bought the buildings where his restaurants are located and paid off the mortgages years ago. He's 70 years old now but carries two cell phones with him at all times. He works like a dog! "But for what?" I ask him. "How much do you need? One day you'll have a heart attack. You have enough money and sufficient cash flow to sustain yourself as well as the next few generations of your family. Stop working so hard and enjoy life a little—enjoy life a lot!"

Historically, mortgage institutions have encouraged investors to take a leveraged position in the real estate market. Unfortunately, too much leverage makes an investment highly prone to fail. The rules of the new economy dictate that you rethink this outdated investment philosophy. Acquire real estate with less leverage and pay off those mortgages. The most successful investors I know buy real estate with a minimal amount of debt and make a concerted effort to pay down those mortgages as soon as possible. Take a more conservative approach to investing, and finance with low leverage and pay down the existing debt as quickly as possible. Cash is, indeed, king, and cash flow is maximized when servicing debt is no longer a factor.

In general, the people I know who are raised without a safety net tend to work much harder in life than those who were raised with a safety net. Having the capacity and desire to consistently work hard is really a gift. Many people don't have the ability to dedicate themselves 100 percent to their chosen vocation. For instance, if you feel that everything can be taken away from you if you fail and no one (parents, uncles, aunts, family friends, etc.) is there to get you out of trouble should you stumble, survival becomes a basic instinct that forces you to work much harder than everyone else. Regardless of your particular station in life, work hard toward your goals—as if you didn't have a safety net and as if failure were not an option. Paying off those mortgages helps, too.

22

The Economic Recovery

An astute real estate investor I know recently commented, "The economy will recover when the press declares it so—and not a day earlier!"

The media's predictions, however, regarding the economic recovery are rather mixed at this time. Many analysts have declared that we reached the bottom in mid- to late 2009, while others claim it will take more time. Some say the recovery will be "V"-shaped while others claim it will be "U"-shaped. The real pessimists predict that shortly after the economy shows signs of recovery, it will be followed by a downturn with high inflation and, perhaps, another recession. An "N"-shaped recovery—up, down, up.

According to a recent *New York Times* article, "60 percent of Americans think the country is heading in the wrong direction, and the same percentage believes that the United States is in long-term decline." Eight million jobs were lost during the past few years, and it's going to be a long climb up the economic ladder to get those jobs back. According to a recent *New York Times* article, "More than 80 percent [of economists] say the United States won't regain all the jobs lost in the recession until 2013 or later." (David Brooks, "Relax, We'll Be Fine," *New York Times,* April 5, 2010, available at http://topics. nytimes.com/top/opinion/editorialsandoped/columnists/davidbrooks/ html?inline=nyt-per; and see also Paul Davidson and Barbara Hansen, "Economists Say Recovery Looks Stronger Than Expected," *USA Today*, July 23, 2010, available at http//www.usatoday.com/money/ economy/2010-0-26-econsurvey26_ST_N.htm.

Admittedly, this economic meltdown has been the worst financial crisis since the Great Depression. But rest assured that an economic rebound will eventually occur, and investors who choose to align themselves on the side of prosperity will act before the media begin writing about the Great Recovery. After all, contrarian investors will have acquired much of the low-hanging real estate fruit in your farm area by the time the media decide to stick their necks out and publicly declare the end of the "Great Recession."

Housing Values and the Recovery

Few economists and housing experts would object to the notion that the recovery of the housing market is paramount to the health of the overall economy. In fact, until housing values bounce back, the recession (in one form or another) will likely continue to plague our nation.

The pace of the housing recovery will vary throughout the country because homes in cities such as Miami, San Diego, Las Vegas, Phoenix, Los Angeles, and Detroit will require significantly more time to regain their value than less hard-hit cities such as Boston, New York, Washington, D.C., and Seattle. Home prices have decreased by as much as 55 percent since the peak of the market. It might take 5 to 10 years for many homeowners to regain the equity lost in their properties. Some property owners might have to wait even longer. Millions of homeowners who owe more on their homes than the homes are currently worth will be confronted with years of negative equity, thereby increasing their risk of foreclosure and adding to the burgeoning supply of distressed real estate that already exists.

Even after home values stop falling, it will take time for some property owners to generate any significant equity. Carrying a property with negative equity will affect the consumer confidence of millions of people. I estimate that as many as 35 percent of property owners' home loans are "under water."

Nevertheless, there are some signs that the housing market is strengthening. Home sales have increased, and the available inventory on the market is gradually shrinking. As mentioned, the latest Case-Shiller report suggests that housing prices bottomed out in 2009.

The overall health of the economy and in particular the housing market is dependent on several factors, including: interest rates, inflation, the credit markets, consumer sentiment, the labor market, and so on.

Jobs and the Recovery

A significant reduction in the unemployment rate will help sustain a strong recovery. But even when the economy does begin to rebound, the unemployment rate might not realize a meaningful improvement because of the enormous number of layoffs during the past few years. And once individuals find gainful employment, their depleted savings will leave them more vulnerable than ever before. You should expect modest employment growth during the next few years (a "jobless recovery"), as most businesses remain reluctant to add additional head count to their payrolls until there's a clear indication of a turnaround.

Companies will avoid hiring as long as possible. Maximizing productivity will be the primary focal point for most firms in the coming years. Because of this, existing employees will be required to be more productive and perform more work than ever before.

Nevertheless, there are indications that employment is improving. Job postings (online listings of job opportunities) rose by nearly 20 percent in 2010, according to Indeed.com. In particular, employers are becoming more bullish in towns such as Boston, San Francisco, New York, and Washington, D.C.

Consumer Confidence and the Recovery

If employment numbers increase in a meaningful way, consumer confidence will rise, and spending will follow. Homeowners will still need to reconfigure their finances after absorbing severe declines in the values of their properties. A psychological reset will need to occur whereby the debt-laden ways of the past are discarded, and a new sense of financial responsibility and accountability will be imprinted on the minds of the next generation. Households will save more than they have in the past, and eventually consumer confidence will be restored. It will, however, take a generation to forget what happened in this meltdown.

The Credit Crunch and the Recovery

The constricted credit markets will impair businesses and investors for years. Businesses will no longer have access to easy loans and unlimited credit. Homebuyers and real estate investors will be confronted with significantly more challenging financial restrictions and will be required to contribute more of their own capital to their acquisitions.

With little to no equity remaining in millions of homes throughout the country, homeowners will be unable to extract capital (in the form of home equity lines) from their homes. This, for the record, is one of the most beneficial outcomes of the economic bust.

Commercial real estate is the next shoe to drop, and lenders are sensitive to the next wave of defaults. They are reining in lending because they realize they're not out of the woods yet. Unfortunately, if banks aren't actively lending, the recovery will take longer to gain momentum.

Interest Rates and the Recovery

Some economists are concerned that heavy government spending along with higher deficits will eventually force interest rates to increase. As interest rates rise, the cost of borrowing for both consumers and businesses becomes more expensive, thereby delaying the recovery.

Reasons to Be Optimistic

During the next 40 years, our country's population is expected to increase by 100 million people. By the year 2050, 400 million people will reside in the United States. This magnitude of population growth, assuming estimates are accurate, will increase exponentially—the demand for apartments, single-family homes, retail centers, offices, hotels, and industrial buildings.

Keep your eye on home prices, GDP growth, the unemployment rate, inflation, retail spending, and the consumer confidence index. There is a host of other economic factors to consider, but these six are the leading indicators, in my opinion, of the economic recovery. On a less scientific basis, I also like to speak with local furniture store owners. Furniture stores are akin to the canary in a coalmine. Their sales (or lack thereof) are an economic barometer during tough times. They tend to be a fairly accurate indicator of the relative health of the local markets.

The Future

We are a country with enormous untapped potential. Regardless of what the pundits might want you to believe, America is still a dynamic and vibrant nation with a bright future ahead of it. Your hard-earned investment dollars are well spent in a place with political stability, relatively fluid financial markets, a rising population, a productive and entrepreneurial workforce, and a history of successfully rebounding from challenging economic times.

Investors willing to embrace risk during precarious economic times will be rewarded. However, once those market risks have subsided, the potential returns will diminish as well. This is the time to invest.

Conclusion

*The flaws in human nature are such that this
sort of crisis will occur again. Maybe not in a
long time, but greed will cause a financial
crisis again.*

—ALAN GREENSPAN

Times have changed. The economy has changed. Financing has
changed. Real estate has changed. Therefore, your strategy for
investing must change.

The terms "housing bubble," "housing crash," and "subprime
mortgage" may not have been part of your everyday vocabulary a few
years ago, but they certainly have become commonly used phrases
today.

The U.S. economy experienced the worst economic recession since
the Great Depression. Subprime lending and too much debt caused the
meltdown, but Wall Street financiers and the federal government per-
petuated it. Fortunes were made during the housing boom, and fortunes
have been subsequently lost during the housing bust. Too much lending
to people who could ill afford the heavy debt pushed the system over the

edge. Unlike the last major economic collapse, when large commercial real estate investors were mostly affected, the average "Joe Citizen" this time around lost his home, savings, and job.

Every time you think you know the rules of the game, the rules change. Now the economy and the real estate markets are shifting into a new phase. The economy will reset, and the rules of engagement will be altered. In the new economy, banks will be more cautious and reluctant to lend unless the risks are significantly minimized. Consumers will be more cautious and spend less (and maybe even save more) until they feel more secure about their jobs. Household debt was reduced by approximately $600 billion since the fall of 2008, according to Equifax. That's proof that households are paying down their debt (i.e., household deleveraging), and it's a positive sign for increased spending power in the future.

The recession, by many estimates, ended in late 2009, and economists appear to be increasingly bullish about the housing market in the next few years. Warren Buffett even predicted the recovery of the residential real estate market by 2011: "Prices will remain far below 'bubble' levels, of course, but for every seller or lender hurt by this, there will be a buyer who benefits. Indeed, many families who couldn't afford to buy an appropriate home a few years ago now find it well within their means." (Bloomberg, March 1, 2010).

Nevertheless, many borrowers will have a difficult time securing mortgages because of tougher standards being imposed by banks. NINJA loans (no income, no job and no assets) have been dismissed as an unethical and unacceptable way of conducting business. Not only will you need to provide evidence of a job, good credit, and a stable source of income, but you will be required to make a sizable down payment for your purchase. New federal laws that prohibit lenders from interacting with appraisers will reduce fraudulent appraisals. It's going to be much more difficult to obtain a loan in the new economy.

High loan-to-value (LTV) ratios coupled with secondary financing are also relics of the past. Our country was addicted to leverage, but we

Conclusion

are now in a period of deleveraging. Property owners who borrowed too much and need to refinance will be required to make substantial equity payments toward their debt to reduce their LTV ratios. Exorbitant leverage made popular in the United States, however, is not an acceptable practice throughout the entire world. In fact, one of my good friends represents a real estate investment fund in Bogotá, Colombia. This firm has no tolerance for purchasing properties with more than 50 percent leverage. In other words, it would need $25 million for a $50 million purchase. Because of Colombia's historical boom and bust cycles, investors in that country realize that they must buy with a significant amount of equity. Most investors who survive the longest and thrive for several decades tend to be more conservative with their real estate financing. They either tap into their own cash reserves or work with well-financed equity partners to acquire real estate with a reasonable amount of debt. They fully understand the threat of using too much debt, so they structure their deals accordingly.

It's back to the basics with sound lending practices, larger down payments, and conventional fixed loans. And don't plan on banks' relaxing their lending standards for quite some time.

"Pigs get fed and hogs get slaughtered," said one of my good friends who heads up the special assets department at a large privately held bank. In other words, if you're a pig, you want to eat but not get so fat as to become a candidate for slaughter at hog-killing time. Politicians who get too greedy can suffer a similar fate at voting time, and the same holds true for investors. If you're overleveraged and wait too long in the cycle to make more money (because of greed), you will eventually get slaughtered.

Both investors and lenders used little discretion. Banks made poor decisions, and investors got caught up in the euphoria. Residential market lending has reverted back to the old rules of lending: 720 credit scores and 20 percent down—and it's a problem if the property's appraisal determines that it's worth less than the purchase price.

Conclusion

In order to make money in this market, it really will take money! There's no free ride anymore.

According to my friend in special assets, "Investors will need a longer-term plan to make $1 million. It's going to be much more difficult to make a million in 12 months. Investors will need to hold properties for their cash flow and pay down debt. They'll be able to sell for a profit down the road but there are no quick profit deals anymore. There are no instant home runs. Instead, there's a lot of hard work and a 5- to 7-year horizon to exit."

When to Buy

Have you ever said to yourself, "When the next recession hits, I'm going to have funds at my disposal to take advantage of some of those great deals"?

Real estate can be a tremendous investment vehicle if you are able to sustain a long-term vision, especially if you buy at depressed prices and have patient money. You need to invest when the sky is falling, and in many parts of the country it has been for years. By the time the media claim that the economy is recovering, the market has already adjusted so don't wait to read about it online. Novice investors jump into the fray when real estate investing is most popular, but the true professionals enter when everyone is frightened by its predicted collapse. That's precisely why novice investors usually get burned, but the experts make a killing.

With debt not readily available and billions of dollars worth of commercial loans maturing, retail and office properties will soon experience their worst years since 1990. Refinancing of commercial mortgages will be nearly impossible unless there's significant equity in the property. But because valuations have come down so much, most loan-to-value covenants have been broken, and refinancing won't be an option for many owners. The entire commercial sector will soften during the next few years, and this will present even more opportunities for savvy investors.

There is undoubtedly an abundance of opportunities to purchase good cash-flowing properties in your farm area. There is also a tremendous opportunity to acquire foreclosures at undervalued prices. However, distressed investing will require extensive due diligence and research on your behalf to avoid overpaying in a market that's continuously evolving. As I've written in all my other books, "You make money when you buy!" Buying well today improves the likelihood that you'll sell profitably in the future.

Real Estate Investing Is a Local Business

A partner at a large accounting firm I do business with told me that a high-net-worth client of his had five commercial loans with his local bank. The firm had always been current on its loans and never posed a financial risk to its lender. The president of this lending institution called him a few months ago to inquire about his appetite for acquiring a property that would complement his existing portfolio—but at a steep discount to its existing debt and well under market value. Because he had been a loyal customer who had always paid his mortgages on time, he was on the bank's priority list to call when distressed deals presented themselves. The moral of the story is that you need to establish strong ties with local lenders, and always make sure they know you are ready to buy.

Success and Optimism

There is a multitude of reasons to explain why some entrepreneurs make it and others fail. Being an entrepreneur is not easy. Some entrepreneurs just fall short of their goals. Success is largely determined by individual characteristics that propel the best entrepreneurs to the pinnacle of achievement.

Conclusion

Ultimately, making money in real estate is less dependent on geography, recessions, recoveries, buyer or seller's markets, REOs, short sales, the credit crunch, lax lending standards, or your personal cash reserves or lack thereof. The most important factor in determining your success is (you guessed it) *you*.

Your success is determined by whether you're a pessimist or an optimist. After all, this book has shown you some ways to make money in real estate, but it's entirely your responsibility to execute a plan and achieve your desired outcome.

Every successful person I know has one trait in common: Each is utterly consumed by positive thinking, and they all are supremely optimistic individuals. They take absolutely nothing for granted. They don't assume that the world owes them great wealth, fame, or success. Life is not fair, so they set their expectations accordingly.

Uber-successful people go out and earn their keep every single day. They tend not to act entitled, and never stop moving forward to achieve their goals. They encounter challenges and difficulties along the way (just like you and me), but they never falter. That's what sets them apart from everyone else. They persevere when others give up. They always find a way to work through problems that otherwise might impede their progress. The word "can't" just isn't part of their vocabulary.

To really believe in your life's mission, you can't be cynical. Skeptical, sure, that's OK, but doubting yourself and blaming others will get you nowhere in life. Don't make excuses, either: I didn't graduate from Harvard; my parents aren't well-connected; I don't have enough experience; and so on. It's far too easy to find reasons for your failure, so just don't do it. People tend to fall short of reaching their dreams and aspirations because they give up too soon. They fail in their commitment to themselves and their life's goals. Successful people stay the course and never waiver. They don't give up or call it quits.

I wish you a great deal of success with the endeavors you are pursuing.

Conclusion

As for my two young boys, I hope this book helped you to better understand your dad. I shall always be by your side rooting for your success and happiness as you travel through this journey called life! TQM

If you have any questions or simply want to share your thoughts with the author, please contact him through his Web site: www.matthewamartinez.com.

Index

Index

Index

Index

Index

Index

Index

Index

Index

Index

About the Author

Matthew Martinez is a principal of Beacon Hill Property Group, a founder of Landlord and Investor Group (LIG), and the author of the bestsellers *2 Years to a Million in Real Estate* and *Investing in Apartment Buildings*. Visit Matthew Martinez online at www.matthewamartinez.com.